Prayer STORM

Study Guide

Prayer STORM

STUDY GUIDE

The Hour That Changes the World

JAMES W. GOLL

DESTINY IMAGE® PUBLISHERS, INC.
P.O. Box 310, Shippensburg, PA 17257-0310

"Speaking to the Purposes of God for this Generation and for the Generations to Come."

This book and all other Destiny Image, Revival Press, Mercy Place, Fresh Bread, Destiny Image Fiction, and Treasure House books are available at Christian bookstores and distributors worldwide.

For a U.S. bookstore nearest you, call 1-800-722-6774.
For more information on foreign distributors, call 717-532-3040.
Reach us on the Internet at www.destinyimage.com.

ISBN 10: 0-7684-2717-7
ISBN 13: 978-0-7684-2717-2

For Worldwide Distribution, Printed in the U.S.A.

1 2 3 4 5 6 7 8 9 10 11 / 12 11 10 09 08

DEDICATION

As a student of Church history and one who loves prayer and its role in world missions, I dedicate this book to the legacy of Count Nicolas Ludwig von Zinzendorf, Christian David, Anna Nitschmann, and the other early leaders of the group that eventually became known as the Moravians. I have been impacted immeasurably by the shadow of the Lord Jesus that they cast. It is an honor to be one of the many intercessors who today have picked up the baton of prayer that the Moravian believers so faithfully carried for well over a hundred years.

ACKNOWLEDGMENTS

With deep, heart-felt gratitude, I wish to thank the team of people at Encounters Network and Destiny Image who made this project possible. I especially want to recognize Kathy Deering as one of the best writing editors I have ever met. It is an honor to work with her.

I also want to say "thank you" to the Holy Spirit for giving me a dream concerning the Prayer Storm and to the Lord for trusting me with a commission to this great task. Thanks to all the prayer warriors who have already joined us in this "hour that changes the world" and to all of you who, after reading this book, will be ready to join in. Together, in Jesus, we make a great team!

ENDORSEMENTS

My dear friend James Goll has been given a mandate that all of us have been called to participate in. It is a call to perpetual unceasing prayer...sounds like God to me. God has given James many prophetic visions and dreams; this one could not have come at a more crucial time in our culture and in our history. The Church is in desperate need of authenticity and relevance...we will find it first on our faces before God. The youth of the world are being visited by God in a fresh way. This will intensify as we pray because the demonic attack against the youth of our generation is unprecedented, and we need to push back the forces of darkness. The descendants of Abraham are in need of Messiah; our prayers on their behalf and our intercession will make a difference. And finally, the world is in a state of turmoil, upheaval, and crisis; only prayer changes the destiny of nations. Our mandate is James' mandate...the Moravian Lampstand must be restored. Once again, my deepest thanks to a man of his word, a man of God's Word, and my brother in arms, James Goll, for being brave enough and bold enough to call us to our highest place of power...our knees!

Dr. Mark J. Chironna
The Master's Touch International Church
Mark Chironna Ministries
Orlando, Florida

James Goll has done it again! His new book, *Prayer Storm*, is a spiritual manual for every Christian, whether new to prayer or an experienced intercessor. This textbook probes the spirit of the early Moravian intercessors and casts a vision for rekindling their powerful lamp into our dark world. James has provided us with principles and sound doctrine, but he also gives us sample prayers and guidelines to become part of a global prayer storm. We learn how to conspire with God to bring His will to come on this earth. We find out how to pray with God instead of praying to God.

James is not starting a new organization that replicates other prayer ministries, but he provides the connecting lines between the dots of intercession around the world. I encourage every Christian to not just read the text contained within this book's pages but to actively participate in a prayer movement that will change our globe.

Harry R. Jackson Jr.
Senior Pastor, Hope Christian Church
Founder and President, High Impact Leadership Coalition
Washington, D.C.

In his newest book, James Goll issues an urgent challenge to every believer to be part of spiritual "crisis intervention" at this critical juncture in history. Through a dream, God revealed a vision and strategy for a worldwide, corporate call to consistent, persistent prayer—Prayer Storm—that will intervene and change things in the earth realm. Four specific areas are targeted for focused prayer. I encourage you to get this book: read it, sign up, and *pray*!

Jane Hansen Hoyt
President/CEO, Aglow International
Edmonds, Washington

I am passionately excited about Jim Goll's powerful book, *Prayer Storm*, that I believe God will use to transform the global prayer movement. Nothing I know of will impact the nations for Jesus Christ like restoring the Moravian Prayer Watch as described in Goll's inspired and anointed call to continuous prayer. Our ministry, Every Home for Christ, wants to be first in line to partner with Jim in this global call to continuous prayer.

Dr. Dick Eastman
International President
Every Home for Christ and
President of America's National
Prayer Committee

A Global Prayer Army is arising in this hour across the face of the earth to lay seize to the kingdom of darkness by penetrating it with the arsenal of worship and intercession. I encourage you to join in the strategic ministry of James W. Goll and countless others worldwide in the Prayer Storm efforts to keep the fire continually burning on the altar. May the fire of the Lord burn on your heart as you read this contagious book.

Lou Engle
Director of The Call

God's heart cry is that His people stand united as watchmen together is this critical hour of history. Join James Goll, myself and thousands of others as we lift our voices for the youth, Israel and the church. We need a revival that brings reformation and only sustained, united prayer will bring this about!

Robert Stearns
Founder of Eagles' Wings
Co-Chairman, Day of Prayer for the Peace of Jerusalem

With a passion for prayer and the purposes of God, James Goll brings us additional needed tools for the global prayer army for these Last Days. I exhort you to be a practical part of the world wide prayer movement and consider joining James Goll and thousands of others in the "hour that changes the world."

Mike Bickle
Director of International House of Prayer of Kansas City
Author of *Passion of Jesus* and many others

The key to sustained revival that transforms society is the power of enduring prayer. The teaching and the applications of *Prayer Storm* will help the global army of intercessors stay focused and targeted in their prayer efforts. Don't just read another book—do what this book says. Have a life full of life- altering intercession.

Dutch Sheets
Senior Leader of Freedom Church
Founder of USAAN
Author of *Intercessory Prayer, Watchmen Prayer*
and Praying for America

Contents

Foreword. 17

Preface 19

Part I   **Vision for a Prayer Storm**. 21

Lesson 1   "Prayer Storm"—What Is It? 23

Lesson 2   Walking in the Footsteps of Jesus. 35

Part II   **Power for a Prayer Storm**. 45

Lesson 3   Spirit-Empowered Prayer Storm 47

Lesson 4   Intercessory Prayer Storm in Times of Crisis 57

Lesson 5   Prayer With Fasting—God's Way 69

Lesson 6   Soaking in His Presence 83

Lesson 7   Tapping the Power of High Praise 91

Part III   **Patterns for a Prayer Storm** 101

Lesson 8   Prayer for Revival in the Church 103

Lesson 9   Prayer for Another Great Awakening—Youth 115

Lesson 10   Praying Your Family Into the Kingdom. 123

Lesson 11   Praying for People in Authority 133

Lesson 12   Praying Effectively for Israel 143

Answers to Reflection Questions 153

Appendixes **157**

Appendix A   Prayer Storm. 159

Appendix B   Resources for Intercessors 163

Endnotes. 169

About the Author 173

FOREWORD

Prayer Storm may well turn out to be one of the most significant messages to the Body of Christ in this season. I will explain so that you will be able to see this book in its full context.

The biblical agenda item that God has been pushing to the top of the priority list of Christian leaders nationally and internationally during this season has been the "Dominion Mandate." Think about Adam and Eve. After God had created all the incredible things on earth, He climaxed it with creating human beings in His own image. Why did God create humans? He created humans so they would take charge of all the rest of creation. God specifically said that Adam and Eve should "take dominion" over what He had put on earth (see Genesis 1:26,28). This is where the term Dominion Mandate originates.

Keep in mind that *Adam* is not only the name of a person, but in Hebrew it means "the human race." You and I were not in the Garden of Eden personally, but we were there genetically because we all have some of Adam's DNA. When Adam acted, he acted not only on his own behalf, but in the broad sense, on our behalf as well. As we know, he definitely made the wrong choice.

Satan knew that God had given Adam the authority to take dominion and also the authority to give dominion away. Satan tempted Adam because he wanted to regain the authority he lost when he was cast out of Heaven. Adam yielded to temptation; he chose to obey satan rather than God, and from that point on satan usurped Adam's rightful dominion and began to have his way in the world, which is to steal, kill, and destroy. That is why satan is called "the god of this age" and "the prince of the power of the air" (see Eph. 2:2).

But this was not and never has been God's plan for life on earth. God turned things around by sending the Second Adam, Jesus Christ. Jesus came to destroy the works of satan, namely to begin the process of taking back the dominion that Adam had given away in the Garden. Jesus sent His disciples out to preach the gospel of the kingdom. *Kingdom* means dominion because it has two parts: *king* and *dom*, which are the first three letters of the word *dominion*. A king has dominion over a realm. Jesus is the King and His realm is the earth. Jesus paid the price for retaking dominion by His death and resurrection. But when He left the earth, He said that we, His disciples, would receive power when the Holy Spirit comes, in order to be His witnesses. What does this mean? Implementing the Dominion Mandate is our responsibility as Jesus' representatives in this season.

Which brings me to the crucial importance of *Prayer Storm*.

James Goll knows and teaches everything I have just said. One thing he knows very well is that when Jesus came to bring His kingdom, He was invading the kingdom that satan had dominated since the time of Adam. What does this mean? It means war! Satan never lets go of any territory he has occupied without a fight. As Jesus' witnesses, it is our responsibility to engage satan and fight this war under the power of the Holy Spirit on Jesus' behalf. The war will not be over until God's people regain their rightful dominion over creation and Jesus turns the kingdom over to His Father as it says in First Corinthians 15:24.

If we are going to win this war, our first weapon must be prayer. I am not referring to the traditional, routine, plain vanilla, religious prayer that most Christians are used to. I mean an extraordinary level of prayer—a battle-winning, world-changing kind of prayer. I mean prayer that will defeat the enemy in your personal life as well as in your church life, as well as seeing the community in which you live transformed for God!

How do we get to this level of prayer? James Goll has drawn on his extensive experience, his profound knowledge of the Word of God, and his fine-tuned spiritual discernment to give us definitive answers to this question in *Prayer Storm*. Yes, *Prayer Storm* is one of the most significant messages to the Body of Christ for this season. As you read, you will find your place in serving God during the wonderful times in which we live!

C. Peter Wagner, Presiding Apostle
International Coalition of Apostles

PREFACE

Restoring the Global Moravian Lampstand

In the spring of 2007, I had a vivid dream. I would call it a "commissioning dream," because in this dream I heard an audible voice utter these words: "I commission you to restore and release the global Moravian lampstand!"

With that imperative sentence ringing in my ears, I woke up. There in my bedroom, in amber-colored letters, I saw two words written out in front of my eyes: *Prayer Storm*.

I was fully awake. Suddenly it was as if God's Spirit downloaded into my spirit what this meant. Intuitively, I knew that Prayer Storm would be a worldwide call to consistent, persistent prayer and that it would involve four expressions of prayer. Prayer Storm would focus on three particular areas, vitally undergirded by a fourth. Prayer Storm would involve prayer for (1) revival in the Church, (2) the greatest youth awakening that the world has ever seen, and (3) Israel, all the descendants of Abraham. These prayers would be strengthened by widespread, well-coordinated intercession for (4) God's intervention in times of major crisis.

This was not a commissioning only for one man; it was a commissioning for many people, for the task of orchestrating a worldwide symphony of worship and prayer. Each person who became involved would have a particular part to play. Prayer Storm would become one more part of the divine tapestry of the prayer movement. With an increasingly effective Internet presence, Prayer Storm could become an international, virtual house of prayer.

Immediately after that dream, my ministry, Encounters Network, set up a website (www.prayerstorm.com). We began to expand on each of the four categories of prayer and to make it possible for people to sign up for specific times of prayer. One hour per person per week—that is all it takes to keep the watch going. It doesn't matter what time zone a person lives in. A global house of prayer spans all of them.

Weekly e-mail communications are one of the many practical tools that we provide for our intercessors. In these, I provide teaching and insight for ongoing prayer. As needed, we release prayer news bulletins when a significant crisis occurs somewhere in the world. Through all the crisis praying, I want to be able to keep us focused though on praying for revival in the Church, a youth awakening, and Israel on an on-going basis. On our weekly Prayer Storm web-based television show, we can actually intercede together. We will inform our community of intercessors via our mailing list whenever the Spirit initiates something new that we feel we should participate in. We want to respond to the progressive vision as it unfolds and to make it possible for you to respond to God's call.

Here we are today, at the beginning of the 21st century, and more and more groups are catching the vision for sustained prayer, worship, and intercession—24/7, unceasing prayer for cities, nations, and the entire globe. I believe that Prayer Storm will raise one more unified, God-ordained voice in the worldwide chorus. In the Garden of Gethsemane, Jesus said to Peter and the other disciples, "Could you not watch with me one hour?" (Matt. 26:40 NKJV). I hear Him asking each one of us that question. Can you watch with Him one hour? Prayer Storm can help you do it. Prayer Storm might just be the hour that changes the world!

A Prayer Storm is on the horizon, and we will be the Storm Warriors. We're going to be prayer warriors who pray in the storm. Do you want to be a part of God's Prayer Storm army? Then this study guide was prepared just for you!

Instructional Guidelines

Reference Materials

This *Prayer Storm Study Guide* has been prepared with your individual, small group, or training center needs in mind. The lessons have been coordinated with the book, *Prayer Storm: The Hour That Changes the World*, published by Destiny Image.

PART I: VISION FOR A PRAYER STORM

Lesson 1: "Prayer Storm"—What Is It?

Lesson 2: Walking in the Footsteps of Jesus

PART II: POWER FOR A PRAYER STORM

Lesson 3: Spirit-Empowered Prayer Storm

Lesson 4: Intercessory Prayer Storm in Times of Crisis

Lesson 5: Prayer With Fasting—God's Way

Lesson 6: Soaking in His Presence

Lesson 7: Tapping the Power of High Praise

PART III: PATTERNS FOR A PRAYER STORM

Lesson 8: Prayer for Revival in the Church

Lesson 9: Prayer for Another Great Awakening—Youth

Lesson 10: Praying Your Family Into the Kingdom

Lesson 11: Praying for People in Authority

Lesson 12: Praying Effectively for Israel

At the end of each lesson, you will find Reflection Questions to help you in your review of the materials that you have studied. (The answers to the Reflection Questions can be found at the end of the study guide.)

Part I

VISION FOR A PRAYER STORM

"Prayer Storm"—What Is It?

As I looked, behold, a stormy wind came out of the north, and a great cloud with a fire enveloping it and flashing continually; a brightness was about it and out of the midst of it there seemed to glow amber metal, out of the midst of the fire (Ezekiel 1:4 AMP).

I. **Definition of Prayer Storm**

 A. Definition of *prayer*

  1. Spoken or unspoken communication with God.

  2. An earnest, heartfelt request made before God, a request conveyed by means of petition.

  3. A religious service at which prayers are said.[1]

 B. Definition of *storm* (noun/verb)

  1. (n.) A disturbance in the air above the earth with strong winds and usually also with rain, snow, sleet, hail, and sometimes lightning and thunder.

  2. (n.) A heavy bombardment of solid objects.

  3. (n.) A sudden, strong outpouring of feeling in reaction to something, for example, of protest or laughter, a torrent of communication.

  4. (v.) To attack or capture a place, especially a well-defended one, suddenly and with great force.

  5. (v.) To be or to go somewhere violently, noisily, and/or angrily.

  6. (v.) To blow strongly, to drop large amounts of precipitation.[2]

C. Scriptures about storms:

He covers His hands with the lightning, and commands it to strike the mark (Job 36:32).

See, the storm of the Lord will burst out in wrath, a whirlwind swirling down on the heads of the wicked. The anger of the Lord will not turn back until He fully accomplishes the purposes of His heart. In days to come you will understand it clearly (Jeremiah 23:19-20 NIV).

Like fire that burns the forest and like a flame that sets the mountains on fire, so pursue them with Your tempest and terrify them with Your storm (Psalm 83:14-15).

The Lord is slow to anger and great in power; the Lord will not leave the guilty unpunished. His way is in the whirlwind and the storm, and clouds are the dust of His feet (Nahum 1:3 NIV).

D. Definition of *intercession, intercede* (Latin/Greek/Hebrew)

1. Latin roots: *inter* (between, among, involved) and *cedere* (to yield, to go, to move, to pay the price of).[3]

   a. In other words, *intercede* means "to go between, as when stepping between someone and his enemy in battle, to stand in the gap, to give an opportunity for a solution to be reached."

   b. *Intercede* means to yield oneself to help those who are weak and who need assistance, to create a pause or an atmospheric shift that holds tumult at bay temporarily.

   c. *Intercede* means to move in the direction of involvement regarding the hurts and needs of others, to become a conduit for Kingdom activity. (See the story of the Good Samaritan in Luke 10:25-37.)

   d. To intercede means to be a go-between, to mediate between two parties, to act between two parties with a view to reconcile those who differ or contend with each other, to mediate, to make entreaties.[4]

2. *Intercession/Intercede* in the Greek lexicon

   a. First definition from the Greek: "to light upon a person or a thing, to fall in with, to hit upon a person or a thing, to chance upon something, to encounter unexpectedly."

b. Second definition from the Greek: "to go to or to meet a person, especially for conversation or consultation."[5]

c. New Testament usages of the words *intercede* and *intercession*:

In the same way the Spirit also helps our weakness; for we do not know how to pray as we should, but the Spirit Himself intercedes for us with groanings too deep for words; and He who searches the hearts knows what the mind of the Spirit is, because He intercedes for the saints according to the will of God (Romans 8:26-27).

Therefore He is able also to save forever those who draw near to God through Him, since He always lives to make intercession for them (Hebrews 7:25).

Therefore I exhort first of all that supplications, prayers, intercessions, and giving of thanks be made for all men, for kings and all who are in authority, that we may lead a quiet and peaceable life in all godliness and reverence (1 Timothy 2:1-2 NKJV).

d. Since Jesus ever lives to make intercession and His Spirit lives in us, we need to come into agreement with Him, for "If two of you on earth agree about anything you ask for, it will be done for you by My Father in heaven. For where two or three come together in My name, there am I with them" (Matt. 18:19-20 NIV).

3. Hebrew word for *intercession* (*paga*) appears only a few times in the Old Testament.[6] Each time provides a new slant on the meaning of the word:

a. "To meet"

You meet and spare him who joyfully works righteousness (uprightness and justice), [earnestly] remembering You in Your ways. Behold, You were angry, for we sinned; we have long continued in our sins [prolonging Your anger]. And shall we be saved? (Isaiah 64:5 AMP).

b. "To light upon," as in Genesis 28:10-17, which shows how God's grace works, with our Divine Helper standing by, ready to aid us in our intercession, moving us from our natural ability to His supernatural ability, from our finite ability to His infinite ability, taking hold of situations with us so as to accomplish the will of God.

c. "To fall upon, attack, strike down, cut down," as in First Samuel 22:11-19 and Second Samuel 1:11-16, which show us how the word *paga* can carry a warfare element, indicating the readiness of a soldier to fall upon or attack the enemy at the word of his commander, striking the mark (remember the lightning strikes of Job 36:32) and cutting down the enemy.

d. "Laid upon," as in Isaiah 53:12 (intercession), "He Himself bore the sin of many, and interceded for the transgressors" and in Isaiah 53:6 (laid upon), "All we like sheep have gone astray; we have turned, every one, to his own way; and the Lord has laid on Him the iniquity of us all" (NKJV).

II. Historic Sustained Prayer Movements

A. Jerusalem (1000 B.C.), the tabernacle of David: Under the leadership of King David, night-and-day worship and prayer continued for 33 years and continued into the next generation under King David's son, Solomon. Both kings financed full-time singers and musicians (see 1 Chron. 9:33; 15:16; 23:5; 25:7; 2 Chron. 5:12-13). The Scriptures prophesy a restoration of David's tabernacle (see Acts 15:16).

B. Northern Ireland (A.D. 555), the monastery at Bangor: The founder and senior abbot of a great sixth-century Irish monastery at Bangor was named Comgall. He and his disciple, Columbanus, initiated night-and-day worship with prayers, which continued for over 300 years and from which much missionary zeal arose.

C. Herrnhut, Saxony (1727), the Moravians and the "Moravian lampstand": In 1722, Count Nicolas Ludwig von Zinzendorf was asked by a group of Christians if they could cross the border from Moravia in order to live on his lands in a small community in what today is eastern Germany. He assented, and they settled in a town they called Herrnhut, which means "the Lord's Watch." Zinzendorf himself had always been interested in a life of prayer and devotion to God, and in 1727, he began to lead daily Bible studies for them. A sudden time of revival occurred, which many have called "the Moravian Pentecost."

1. One of the first results of the revival was that 24 young men and 24 young women (all were young; even Zinzendorf was only 27 years old) covenanted to devote one hour every day to concerted, night-and-day prayer. This was the beginning of what became a 100-year-long prayer watch. Every hour of every day, someone was praying.

2. The men and women of Herrnhut committed themselves to hourly intercession in order to, in their own words, "win for the Lamb the rewards of His suffering." They prayed 24 hours a day, 7 days a week, 365 days a year. The "altar fire" never went out. Their fundamental Scripture was, "The fire shall ever be burning upon the altar; it shall never go out" (Lev. 6:13 KJV).

3. This prayer vigil fueled a missionary movement that touched the world. As the years passed, they passed the baton to others; Zinzendorf died in 1760. But the prayer continued unabated.[7]

III. Sustained Prayer Movements Today

A. Seoul, South Korea, the Prayer Mountain: The Osanri Choi Ja-Shil Memorial Fasting Prayer Mountain, Osanri, Kyonggi Province, Korea, was founded by David Yonggi Cho's Yoidi Full Gospel Church of Seoul, South Korea. The Prayer Mountain can accommodate up to 10,000 people at one time for private and corporate prayer.

B. Kansas City, Missouri, International House of Prayer: Mike Bickle and his team coordinate 24/7 worship and intercession, and they sponsor or co-sponsor conferences, webcasts and podcasts, Nightwatch, the Israel Mandate, and the Global Bridegroom Fast.

C. Colorado Springs, Colorado, U.S. Global Apostolic Prayer Network/Strategic Prayer Network: Coordinated by C. Peter Wagner, Chuck Pierce, and Global Harvest Ministries (http://www.globalharvest.org/), the network links committed intercessors who are organized on a national, state, and local level in a concerted effort of global prayer.

D. Charlotte, North Carolina, Watch of the Lord: This is a global prayer movement begun by Mahesh and Bonnie Chavda in 1995. Up to a thousand believers ("watchmen") gather at the watch headquarters in Charlotte, North Carolina, every Friday night to spend the entire night in worship and prayer. Other locations host similar gatherings. Individuals can participate in the Watch of the Lord via Webcast.

E. Many others (see Appendix B, Resources for Intercession), including 24-7 Prayer, Every Home for Christ/Jericho Center of Prayer, Intercessors for America, Jerusalem House of Prayer for All Nations, National Governmental Prayer Alliance, Reformation Prayer Network, and Succat Hallel.

IV. Kingdom of Priests

A. New Testament revelation

1. Royal priesthood

But you are a chosen people, a royal priesthood, a holy nation, a people belonging to God, that you may declare the praises of Him who called you out of darkness into His wonderful light (1 Peter 2:9 NIV).

To Him who loves us and has freed us from our sins by His blood, and has made us to be a kingdom and priests to serve His God and Father—to Him be glory and power for ever and ever! Amen.... You have made them to be a kingdom and priests to serve our God, and they will reign on the earth (Revelation 1:6; 5:10 NIV).

2. Offering up spiritual sacrifices

    a. "Through Him then, let us continually offer up a sacrifice of praise to God, that is, the fruit of lips that give thanks to His name" (Heb. 13:15).

    b. "Enter His gates with thanksgiving and His courts with praise. Give thanks to Him, bless His name" (Ps. 100:4).

    c. Here we find the golden harp and bowl upon the altar in Heaven. The incense of prayer fills the bowl, and the harp represents the ministry of praise and worship. The angel takes his censor, fills it with fire on the altar, and casts it to the earth.

And He came and took the book out of the right hand of Him who sat on the throne. When He had taken the book, the four living creatures and the twenty-four elders fell down before the Lamb, each one holding a harp and golden bowls full of incense, which are the prayers of the saints. And they sang a new song, saying, *"Worthy are You to take the book and to break its seals; for You were slain, and purchased for God with Your blood men from every tribe and tongue and people and nation. You have made them to be a kingdom and priests to our God; and they will reign upon the earth"…Another angel came and stood at the altar, holding a golden censer; and much incense was given to him, so that he might add it to the prayers of all the saints on the golden altar which was before the throne. And the smoke of the incense, with the prayers of the saints, went up before God out of the angel's hand. Then the angel took the censer and filled it with the fire of the altar, and threw it to the earth; and there followed peals of thunder and sounds and flashes of lightning and an earthquake* (Revelation 5:7-10; 8:3-5).

B. Old Testament typology

1. Altar of incense

Moreover, you shall make an altar as a place for burning incense;…Aaron shall burn fragrant incense on it; he shall burn it every morning when he trims the lamps. When Aaron trims the lamps at twilight, he shall burn incense. There shall be perpetual incense before the Lord throughout your generations. You shall not offer any strange incense on this altar, or burnt offering or meal offering (Exodus 30:1,7-9).

Then the Lord said to Moses, "Take for yourself spices, stacte and onycha and galbanum, spices with pure frankincense; there shall be an equal part of each. With it you shall make incense, a perfume, the work of a perfumer, salted, pure, and holy" (Exodus 30:34-35).

Aaron shall enter the holy place with this: with a bull for a sin offering and a ram for a burnt offering….He shall take a firepan full of coals of fire from upon the altar before the Lord and two handfuls of finely ground sweet incense, and bring it inside the veil (Leviticus 16:3,12).

2. Fire on the altar

Command Aaron and his sons, saying, "This is the law for the burnt offering: the burnt offering itself shall remain on the hearth on the altar all night until the morning, and the fire on the altar is to be kept burning on it. The priest is to put on his linen robe, and he shall put on undergarments next to his flesh; and he shall take up the ashes to which the fire reduces the burnt offering on the altar and place them beside the altar. Then he shall take off his garments and put on other garments, and carry the ashes outside the camp to a clean place. The fire on the altar shall be kept burning on it. It shall not go out, but the priest shall burn wood on it every morning; and he shall lay out the burnt offering on it, and offer up in smoke the fat portions of the peace offerings on it. Fire shall be kept burning continually on the altar; it is not to go out (Leviticus 6:9-13).

Moses said to Aaron, "Take your censer and put in it fire from the altar, and lay incense on it; then bring it quickly to the congregation and make atonement for them, for wrath has gone forth from the Lord, the plague has begun!" Then Aaron took it as Moses had spoken, and ran into the midst of the assembly, for behold, the plague had begun among the people. So he put on the incense and made atonement for the people. He took his stand between the dead and the living, so that the plague was checked (Numbers 16:46-48).

3. Four qualities of incense

   a. Stacte is a resinous sap that oozes through the bark of a type of tree that was a day's journey into Syria. In other words, it could only be obtained by walking into enemy territory. It cost the perfumer something to get the stacte. In the same way, it costs us something, and we have to go into enemy territory to gather the "drops," or Word of God, which bubble forth into prophecy. You have to store up the Word within your heart, and then it oozes forth in words of prophetic prayer. It's not an automatic-pilot sort of thing; you have to study to show yourself approved as a workman for God (see 2 Tim. 2:15).

   b. Onycha came from the shell of a mollusk that lived in the Mediterranean Sea. Again, it took some effort to obtain it, because the perfumer had to walk so far. Then it had to be ground into a fine powder and further treated in order to give the incense its sweet odor when it was burned. In a similar way, our lives are to be broken before Him (see Ps. 51:17), and the "fragrance" of our lives offered on the altar is well-pleasing to God. Prayer is made up of an equal portion of the Word and of brokenness in our lives.

   c. *Galbanum* means "richness" or "fatness." Galbanum is a rich gum resin that holds the other ingredients together. Even though it is a bitter substance, it gives important tang to the fragrance, and it reminds us of the bitterness of sin. With the Spirit of Jesus dwelling in us, we possess His rich grace, which we exhibit through lives of faith and praise.

d. We all know about frankincense because it was one of the gifts brought by the Magi to the infant Jesus (see Matt. 2:11). In Old Testament times, it was known as *lavonah*, which means "white." In our prayers, we need the purity and "whiteness" of the righteousness that comes as God's gift to us, not because of our actions, but because of the sacrifice that Jesus accomplished.

4. The requirements for the incense of prayer

a. The ingredients must be gathered from long distances. Developing a true prayer life costs us something and takes time.

b. All four ingredients must be equally balanced. Some people "camp" around the Word, others emphasize brokenness, still others declare the "fatness" message, while others stress holiness and purity. However, we should have a balance of all four.

c. The incense had to be made fresh every day. It could not be made ahead of time. We must pray every day.

d. Fire had to be added to it. We add fervency and zeal to our prayer.

Summary

Worship, pray, and intercede as much as you can, because it is a sweet-smelling fragrance to the Lord, like burning incense in His nostrils.

Reflection Questions

Lesson 1: "Prayer Storm"—What Is It?

(Answers to these questions can be found in the back of the study guide.)

1. A prayer storm is when people _____ out, not quietly but in a passionate, verbal way, asking God, in the name of Jesus, to change things, calling forth the strong winds of the Spirit and the lightnings of His power.

2. The Moravian lampstand refers to the _____ of the incense of prayer on the _____ of God (see Lev. 6:13), which the Moravians in Germany kept burning for over 100 years by night-and-day prayer.

3. The word *intercede* comes from Latin root words _____, which means between, among, involved and _____, which means to yield, to go, to move, to pay the price of. In other words, *intercede* means "to go between, as when stepping between someone and his enemy in battle, to _____ in the gap, to give an opportunity for a solution to be reached.

4. A key Scripture for night-and-day (24/7) worship and prayer is Revelation 5:8: "The four living creatures and the twenty-four elders fell down before the Lamb, each one holding a _____ and golden _____ full of incense, which are the prayers of the saints."

5. The four requirements for the incense of prayer are:

    a. The ingredients must be gathered from long _____.

    b. All four ingredients must be equally_____.

    c. The incense had to be made _____ every day.

    d. _____ had to be added to the incense.

Personal application question

6. Who is smelling the incense of your prayers? Who are you lifting up in prayer on a regular basis?

    _____

    _____

    _____

    _____

    _____

    _____

Lesson 2

WALKING IN THE FOOTSTEPS OF JESUS

"You are a priest forever According to the order of Melchizedek."… He, because He continues forever, has an unchangeable priesthood. Therefore He is also able to save to the uttermost those who come to God through Him, since He always lives to make intercession for them (Hebrews 7:21,24-25 NKJV).

I. **Jesus, Our Magnificent Intercessor**

   A. Christ: three expressions of intercession

   1. Examples from His earthly prayer life

   a. He prayed all night before the choosing of the 12 disciples

It was at this time that He went off to the mountain to pray, and He spent the whole night in prayer to God. And when day came, He called His disciples to Him and chose twelve of them, whom He also named as apostles (Luke 6:12-13).

   b. He was fervent, expressing His prayers loudly and emotionally

In the days of His flesh, He offered up both prayers and supplications with loud crying and tears to the One able to save Him from death, and He was heard because of His piety (Hebrews 5:7).

   c. He was compassionate

When Jesus saw [Mary] sobbing, and the Jews who came with her [also] sobbing, He was deeply moved in spirit and troubled. [He chafed in spirit and sighed and was disturbed.] And He said, Where have you laid him? They said to Him, Lord, come and see. Jesus wept. The Jews said, See how [tenderly] He loved him! But some of them said, Could not He Who opened a blind man's eyes have prevented this man from dying? Now Jesus, again sighing repeatedly and deeply disquieted, approached the tomb. It was a cave (a hole in the rock), and a boulder lay against [the entrance to close] it (John 11:33-38 AMP).

    d.   *Embrimaomai*—"to have indignation on, i.e., to blame, to sigh with chagrin [which implies being distressed],...to groan, to murmur against."[1]

2.   His position at the right hand of God the Father

    a.   *"If anyone sins, we have an Advocate with the Father, Jesus Christ the righteous"* (1 John 2:1b).

    b.   At the right hand of God

Jesus replied, "But I say to all of you: In the future you will see the Son of Man sitting at the right hand of the Mighty One and coming on the clouds of heaven" (Matthew 26:64b NIV).

So then, when the Lord Jesus had spoken to them, He was received up into heaven and sat down at the right hand of God (Mark 16:19).

The Lord says to my Lord: "Sit at My right hand until I make Your enemies a footstool for Your feet" (Psalm 110:1).

...which He brought about in Christ, when He raised Him from the dead and seated Him at His right hand in the heavenly places (Ephesians 1:20).

Therefore if you have been raised up with Christ, keep seeking the things above, where Christ is, seated at the right hand of God (Colossians 3:1).

    c.   Positioned between us and God, the Judge of all

3.   His ongoing activity in Heaven

    a.   "...and to Jesus, the mediator of a new covenant, and to the sprinkled blood, which speaks better than the blood of Abel" (Heb. 12:24).

    b.   Charles Spurgeon said, on the effectiveness of His blood, "Many keys fit many locks, but the master key is the blood and the name of Him that died, and rose again, and ever lives in heaven to save unto the uttermost. The blood of Christ is that which unlocks the treasury of heaven."[2]

    c.   *"He is also able to save to the uttermost those who come to God through Him, since He always lives to make intercession for them"* (Heb. 7:25 NKJV).

B. Christ is our priestly model. Intercession reached its fullest and most profound expression when our sins were "laid upon" Jesus. It is little wonder that the Bible calls it a mystery, hidden deeply within the mind of God. Somehow in the wisdom of God, Jesus was able to identify fully with us, having the totality of our condition placed upon Him. Then, as the scapegoat, He carried it far away. There is an aspect of this form of intercession that we, as His Body, can enter into. It isn't exactly the same as His was, of course, in that His was redemptive in nature. Nonetheless, there is a sharing on behalf of His Body (which is the Church) in filling up that which is lacking in Christ's afflictions (see Col. 1:24).

    1. Prophesied by Isaiah

        a. *"My Servant, will justify the many, as He will bear their iniquities.... because He poured out Himself to death, and was numbered with the transgressors; yet He Himself bore the sin of many, and interceded for the transgressors"* (Isa. 53:11-12).

        b. See Isaiah 53:6,12, which is quoted below in point 4.c.

    2. He humbled Himself

        a. "[He] emptied Himself, taking the form of a bond-servant, and being made in the likeness of men. Being found in appearance as a man, He humbled Himself by becoming obedient to the point of death, even death on a cross" (Phil. 2:7-8).

    3. He took on the sins of mankind

        a. "He made Him who knew no sin to be sin on our behalf, so that we might become the righteousness of God in Him" (2 Cor. 5:21).

        b. "Father, forgive them, for they do not know what they are doing" (Luke 23:34).

    4. He lifts and carries away our transgressions

a. *Nasa* (Hebrew)—"to life up, bear away; remove to a distance."[3] There is joy in taking up a burden and then casting it away.

b. "As far as the east is from the west, so far has He removed our transgressions from us" (Ps. 103:12).

c. *All of us like sheep have gone astray, each of us has turned to his own way; but the Lord has caused the iniquity of us all to fall on Him...Therefore, I will allot Him a portion with the great, and He will divide the booty with the strong; because He poured out Himself to death, and was numbered with the transgressors; yet He Himself bore the sin of many, and interceded for the transgressors* (Isaiah 53:6,12).

II. Our Role as Priestly Burden-Bearers

A. From the Greek lexicon

1. *Bastazo*: A verb that means "to take up with the hands"; "to take up in order to carry or bear"; "to bear what is burdensome"; "to bear, to carry"; "to carry on one's person"; "to sustain, i.e. uphold, support"; "to bear away, carry off."[4]

Now we who are strong ought to bear the weaknesses of those without strength and not just please ourselves. Each of us is to please his neighbor for his good, to his edification. For even Christ did not please Himself; but as it is written, "The reproaches of those who reproached You fell on Me" (Romans 15:1-3).

Bear one another's burdens, and so fulfill the law of Christ (Galatians 6:2 NKJV).

2. *Anechomai*: Greek term translated in the KJV with the words "bear with," "endure," "forbear," and "suffer," and in the NASB with the words "bear," "bearing," "endure," "showing tolerance," and "tolerate." The word can also imply "to stake up," like staking up a weak plant, supporting something so that when the winds of adversity blow, a weak person has extra support.[5]

So, as those who have been chosen of God, holy and beloved, put on a heart of compassion, kindness, humility, gentleness and patience; bearing with one another, and forgiving each other, whoever has a complaint against anyone; just as the Lord forgave you, so also should you (Colossians 3:12-13).

Therefore I...implore you to walk in a manner worthy of the calling with which you have been called, with all humility and gentleness, with patience, showing tolerance for one another in love (Ephesians 4:1-2).

B. The work of Christ

This was to fulfill what was spoken through Isaiah the prophet: "He Himself took our infirmities and carried away our diseases" (Matthew 8:17).

For we do not have a high priest who cannot sympathize with our weaknesses, but One who has been tempted in all things as we are, yet without sin (Hebrews 4:15).

Now all these things are from God, who reconciled us to Himself through Christ and gave us the ministry of reconciliation, namely, that God was in Christ reconciling the world to Himself, not counting their trespasses against them, and He has committed to us the word of reconciliation. Therefore, we are ambassadors for Christ, as though God were making an appeal through us; we beg you on behalf of Christ, be reconciled to God. He made Him who knew no sin to be sin on our behalf, so that we might become the righteousness of God in Him. And working together with Him, we also urge you not to receive the grace of God in vain (2 Corinthians 5:18–6:1).

III. Invited to Participate in the Work of Christ

A. Our Scriptural position in Christ. From our position with Him in Heaven, it is our great joy and honor to intercede for others, to bridge the gap that separates them from His provision. Just as Jesus is our tireless Intercessor, so we keep the fires of intercession burning day and night. It is from our position with Him—not from a position far beneath the clouds—that we seek His intervention. We pray from "up here" to "down there."

1. God has "raised us up with Him, and seated us with Him in the heavenly places in Christ Jesus" (Eph. 2:6).

2. We "have been raised up with Christ, [and we] keep seeking the things above, where Christ is, seated at the right hand of God" (Col. 3:1).

3. Those of us who bear His name, He has called "the priests of the Lord" and "ministers of our God" (Isa. 61:6a).

B. Our authority to call forth "targets" in prayer: intercession releases the flashing forth of His glory, light, or lightning (which covers His hands—see Job. 36:32) and directs it to strike the mark in the desired situation.

C. From Wesley Duewel, *Mighty Prevailing Prayer:*

As enthroned Son of Man, what does Jesus live to do? Does He live to welcome the saints to heaven at their death? I am sure He welcomes them, but the Bible does not say so. Does He live to grant interviews to saints and angels? He most probably does this, but the Bible does not say so. Does He live to enjoy heaven's music? I am sure He thrills to do it. He created us to be able to enjoy music along with Him, but there is something more important than listening to music. Does He live to reign? Most certainly He does—and He will reign for ever and ever.

The Bible emphasizes one role of Jesus today above all others—He is *Priest* forever (Heb. 5:6; 6:20; 7:17,21). His priesthood is permanent (7:24) because He always lives to intercede (v. 25). His sovereign throne is a throne of grace, both because of His atonement and because He ever lives to intercede for us. His is a priestly throne (8:1).

Romans 8:34 associates two facts: Christ at the right hand of God, and Christ interceding for us. What does this intercession for us imply? Many commentators feel that His very presence seated on the throne of heaven is sufficient in itself as a glorious intercession. They doubt that He is actually praying. They feel that He does not need to make any requests of the Father; His sitting on the throne is all the request necessary.

But Jesus is the same yesterday, today, and forever (Heb. 13:8). While on earth, He loved us, yearned for us, and prayed for us (John 17). He prayed for Peter personally (Luke 22:32). As Son of Man, He is as intensely concerned about and interested in each one of us as He ever was. He is still as sympathetic as He ever was (Heb. 4:15). The Greek word used here, *sympatheō,* means "to suffer with." The whole argument of Hebrews 4:15-16 is that we are to come to the throne of grace (where Jesus is interceding) with confidence because He does sympathize and suffer with our pain. He is touched and moved by our need and feels its pain. He feels for us as infinitely as He ever did. His throne of intercession for us is a throne of feeling intercession.[6]

Summary

Jesus' throne is a one of "feeling intercession," and we stand with Him, willing and eager to intercede through Him. We cannot add to what Christ has done, but modeling what He does, we have the burdens and weaknesses of others placed upon us for intercessory purposes. We carry them to the throne, allowing the Holy Spirit to appropriate the benefits of the Cross, acknowledging and receiving the grace of our Lord and the power of His shed blood as sufficient.

Reflection Questions

Lesson 2: Walking in the Footsteps of Jesus

(Answers to these questions can be found in the back of the study guide.)

1. (Review I.A.) Name three expressions of Jesus' intercession.

    _____

    _____

    _____

2. Where is Jesus' position in Heaven? What does this signify?

    _____

    _____

3. Does Jesus intercede with emotion? _____ How do you know?

    _____

    _____

4. Intercession is burden-bearing. There is joy in taking up a _____ and then casting it away.

5. What does it mean to say that we pray from "up here" to "down there"?

    _____

    _____

PERSONAL APPLICATION QUESTIONS

6. What are two prayer-burdens that you have prayed for in the past and have successfully "cast away" as burdens?

_____

_____

7. What are two prayer-burdens that you are carrying to the throne right now?

_____

_____

Part II

POWER FOR A PRAYER STORM

SPIRIT-EMPOWERED PRAYER STORM

"I have heard you," replied Jeremiah the prophet. "I will certainly pray to the Lord your God as you have requested; I will tell you everything the Lord says and will keep nothing back from you" (Jeremiah 42:4 NIV).

I. **What Is Spirit-Empowered Prayer?**

A. Letting the Holy Spirit lead you. (The terms *Spirit-empowered prayer, prophetic intercession,* and *revelatory prayer* are interchangeable.)

1. "All who are being led by the Spirit of God, these are the sons of God" (Rom. 8:14).

2. As in a waltz or dance, you let the other take the lead and gently nudge you in the direction you are to go.

B. Letting the Holy Spirit empower you. In Spirit-empowered prayer, the Holy Spirit will light upon you and give you power, just as it was on the day of Pentecost (see Acts 2). It's like getting a booster to your rocket. Your prayers will hit the target.

II. **The Power of Prophetic Intercession**

A. Prophetic intercession: prophet and priest brought together

1. Priest: pleads the needs of the people to the Lord

2. Prophet: pleads the interests of God before the people

3. Authentic prophetic intercession: priest and prophet unite in their graces and burdens

B. Prophetic intercession pleads the promises

1. As you arise in worship and are seated with Christ Jesus in the heavenly places, you are not just praying to God, but rather, having come into agreement with His heart, you are now praying *with* God.

2. In revelatory prayer, you pave the way for the fulfillment of the prophetic promise that has been revealed previously.

3. In prophetic intercession, the Spirit of God pleads, through the believer, the covenant promises of God that have been made to His people throughout history. Every unfulfilled promise should be pleaded by the Spirit-empowered believer before the throne.

4. Revelatory prayer or prophetic intercession is an urging from the Holy Spirit to pray for situations or circumstances about which you have very little knowledge in the natural.

    a. You pray for the prayer requests that are on the heart of God.

    b. The Spirit nudges you to pray so that He can intervene.

    c. God will direct you to pray in order to bring forth His will on the earth as it is in Heaven.

C. The "Anna Company" (see Luke 2:36-38)

    1. Anna's primary prophetic ministry was her life of prayer, which helped prepare the way for the coming of the Messiah.

    2. As it was in the first coming of Jesus, so it will be before the second coming—gifted, consecrated, prophetic intercessors will lay hold of the purposes of God.

D. Prophetic Intercession = Conspiring

    1. The word *conspire* means "to breathe together." When God created man from the dust of the earth, He breathed into his nostrils the breath of life and man became a living being (see Gen. 2:7). The Hebrew word that we translate "breathed" can mean to breathe violently, such as when the violent, rushing wind filled the upper room on the day of Pentecost.[1]

2. Prophetic intercession is our conspiring (breathing together) with God, breathing violently into situations through prayer in order to bring forth life.

E. Prophetic intercession (Spirit-empowered prayer)—two definitions

1. Prophetic intercession is the ability to receive an immediate prayer request from God and to pray about it in a divinely anointed utterance.

2. Prophetic intercession is waiting before God in order to "hear" or receive God's burden (His Word, His concern, His warning, His conditions, His vision, or His promises) and responding back to the Lord and then to the people with appropriate actions.

III. Forms of Spirit-Inspired Prayer

A. Praying in the Spirit through the gift of tongues

1. Praying with the gift of tongues is one of the foremost forms of Spirit-inspired prayer.

2. Praying in the Spirit is your spirit communicating directly with God. It's called a "prayer language." "For anyone who speaks in a tongue does not speak to men but to God. Indeed, no one understands him; he utters mysteries with his spirit" (1 Cor. 14:2 NIV).

3. Praying in the Spirit is a perfect prayer.

The Spirit helps us in our weakness. We do not know what we ought to pray for, but the Spirit himself intercedes for us with groans that words cannot express. And he who searches our hearts knows the mind of the Spirit, because the Spirit intercedes for the saints in accordance with God's will (Romans 8:26-28 NIV).

For if I pray in an [unknown] tongue, my spirit [by the Holy Spirit within me] prays, but my mind is unproductive [it bears no fruit and helps nobody] (1 Corinthians 14:14 AMP).

a. Since you do not always know how or what to pray in a given situation, you can bring the need before the Lord by praying in the Spirit.

b. Praying in the Spirit is the means by which the Spirit intercedes through your spirit.

4. Praying in the Spirit has definite meaning.

a. Although you do not understand what you are praying, God does. He inspired it, and He also comprehends it.

b. "There are, perhaps, a great many kinds of languages in the world, and no kind is without meaning" (1 Cor. 14:10).

5. Praying in the Spirit edifies the person who is praying.

a. As you use your prayer language consistently, you are built up, strengthened, and encouraged.

b. "One who speaks in a tongue edifies himself" (1 Cor. 14:4a).

c. "But you, dear friends, build yourselves up in your most holy faith and pray in the Holy Spirit" (Jude 20 NIV).

6. Praying in the Spirit has the authority of Heaven behind it.

a. You cannot know in the natural when satan and his demonic forces will launch an attack, but the Holy Spirit will keep you on the alert and prompt you at the opportune time.

b. "The effective prayer of a righteous man can accomplish much" (James 5:16b).

c. "I will pray with the spirit and I will pray with the mind also; I will sing with the spirit and I will sing with the mind also" (1 Cor. 14:15).

d. Like Paul, you can pray and worship in the Spirit. The weapon of perfect prayer and praise is powerful and always on target.

B. Diversities of tongues

Now concerning spiritual gifts, brethren, I would not have you ignorant....Now there are diversities of gifts, but the same Spirit. And there are differences of administrations, but the same Lord. And there are diversities of operations, but it is the same God which worketh all in all. But the manifestation of the Spirit is given to every man to profit withal....Now ye are the body of Christ, and mem-

bers in particular. And God hath set some in the church, first apostles, secondarily prophets, thirdly teachers, after that miracles, then gifts of healings, helps, governments, diversities of tongues (1 Corinthians 12:1,4-7;27-28 KJV).

1. There are different types of tongues. The word translated "diversities" above is the Greek word *genos*, which refers to a collection of different things belonging to the same group or family.[2] (Diversities of tongues are heavenly utterances that differ from each other, yet are related to each other by the Spirit.)

2. Examples of diversities of tongues

    a. Tongues at the filling of the Holy Spirit (See Acts 2:1-4; 10:44-46; Mark 16:17.)

    b. Tongues for interpretation (See First Corinthians 12:7-10; Isaiah 28:11.)

    c. Tongues of edification (See Jude 20 and First Corinthians 14:4.)

    d. Tongues as a sign to the unbeliever (See First Corinthians 14:22.)

    e. Tongues of intercession (See Romans 8:26—the word *groanings* in this verse can be translated as "inarticulate speech," and it refers to speech that does not originate in the intellect or with the understanding, speech that is not related to race or nationality. Inarticulate speech includes, but is not limited to, "other tongues.")[3]

    f. Tongues of warfare (Sometimes the Holy Spirit goes on the offensive. He battles through us. Sometimes He couples together the gift of tongues with the gift of faith or the gift of discerning of spirits. You will feel a rising up inside and a push or an urge to launch out against demonic forces. You attack the powers of darkness, taking authority over satan and rejecting his plans, and you do it by the power of the Holy Spirit who dwells within you. This is your tongue of intercession engaged in warfare, bringing deliverance, healing, and liberty.)

IV. **The Prayer of Groaning and Travail**

   A. Intense, fervent praying

1. "Elijah was a man with a nature like ours, and he prayed earnestly that it would not rain, and it did not rain on the earth for three years and six months. Then he prayed again, and the sky poured rain and the earth produced its fruit" (James 5:17-18).

2. Fervency—to pray with purpose and serious intention. The word *fervent* comes from the Latin word for "to boil; hot."[4]

3. To pray earnestly means that one's entire being is engaged in prayer.

B. Jesus, our example in fervent praying

1. "In the days of His flesh [Jesus] offered up definite, special petitions…and supplications with strong crying and tears" (Heb. 5:7a AMP).

2. "Strong crying and tears," especially the Greek term for it, gives the idea that He cried out loudly in prayer, even shouting and screaming. It was the sound of the battlefield, a struggle of life and death. In no way was it timid or restrained.

C. Laboring in prayer through travail and groaning (see Rom. 8:26-27)

1. The prayer of travail

   a. The prayer of travail is an expression of God's desire to create an opening in order to bring forth a measure of life or growth, just as the opening of a womb is enlarged to bring forth a baby.

   b. If the "opening" were already in place, there would be no need to travail.

The Lord will go forth like a mighty man, He will rouse up His zealous indignation and vengeance like a warrior; He will cry, yes, He will shout aloud, He will do mightily against His enemies. [Thus says the Lord] I have for a long time held My peace, I have been still and restrained Myself. Now I will cry out like a woman in travail, I will gasp and pant together (Isaiah 42:13-14 AMP).

2. The prayer of groaning

   a. Groaning brings deliverance from within and pushes back the pressures of darkness from without. Within each of us are walls of resistance that we cannot see or get free of. This kind of prayer bypasses our understanding and allows the Holy Spirit to move us into the purposes of God.

b.   The prayer of groaning originates deep within our spirits. It is deep calling unto deep. It brings release from the graveclothes of dead works, stripping us so that we might be re-clothed by the Spirit of God. We long for even a foretaste of things to come, and we want to be prepared: "For indeed in this house we groan, longing to be clothed with our dwelling from heaven" (2 Cor. 5:2).

Summary

This kind of prayer takes time and tenacity. We go through stretches when we are not crying out, and when nothing seems to be happening. It's like being a watchman on a wall when nothing is happening. But we don't abandon our post. We need to be ready if the Holy Spirit is ready. We operate with a watchman's anointing, watching to see things in the Spirit. Together with fellow watchers, you maintain the watch.

Reflection Questions

Lesson 3: Spirit-Empowered Prayer Storm

(Answers to these questions can be found in the back of the study guide.)

1. What are two interchangeable terms for *Spirit-empowered prayer?*

    a. _____

    b   _____

2. In prophetic intercession: _____ and _____ are brought together. You perform the functions of both—you plead the needs of the people to the Lord, and you plead the interests of God before the people.

3. Terminology review: Why can we say that prophetic intercession is *conspiring?*

    _____

    _____

4. Praying with the gift of _____ is one of the foremost forms of Spirit-inspired prayer.

5. The prayer of _____ is an expression of God's desire to create an opening in order to bring forth a measure of life or growth, just as the opening of a womb is enlarged to bring forth a baby.

PERSONAL APPLICATION QUESTION

6. In prophetic intercession, the Spirit of God pleads, through you, the covenant promises of God that have been made to His people throughout history, as well as immediate matters. Give an example of each type of prayer:

   a. a covenant promise: _____

   b. an immediate matter: _____

Lesson 4

INTERCESSORY PRAYER STORM IN TIMES OF CRISIS

With all prayer and petition pray at all times in the Spirit, and with this in view, be on the alert with all perseverance and petition for all the saints (Ephesians 6:18).

I. Calling Forth Intervention in Perilous Times

A. Extreme results are preceded by extreme prayer. In every period of history, extreme prayer has been in the forefront of the purposes of God. For every historic revival, people interceded in desperation for God to visit them, change them, and deliver them. How desperate are we, as heavenly ambassadors, on behalf of our families, our churches, and our regions?

B. The shaking and the glory come together.

This is what the Lord Almighty says: "In a little while I will once more shake the heavens and the earth, the sea and the dry land. I will shake all nations, and the desired of all nations will come, and I will fill this house with glory," says the Lord Almighty. "The silver is mine and the gold is mine," declares the Lord Almighty. "The glory of this present house will be greater than the glory of the former house," says the Lord Almighty (Haggai 2:6-9a NIV).

C. Four contributing factors to crisis events in the earth:

1. God's zeal and passion is to remove all that hinders love, to prepare a Bride. Although His role in causing crises is often ignored, He is actively involved. Not all crises are caused by satan or sinful man. Sometimes God allows other forces to work, but sometimes He causes a crisis in a direct way.

2. Satan's rage is permitted by God, within boundaries that He sets. In the culmination of the endtimes, these boundaries will be enlarged (see Rev. 12:12).

3. Man's sin can bring death and destruction to others. We can use our free will for good or for evil.

4. Creation groans and travails. This can be seen in earthquakes, violent weather patterns, etc.

The earth is also defiled under its inhabitants, because they have transgressed the laws, changed the ordinance, broken the everlasting covenant. Therefore the curse has devoured the earth, and those who dwell in it are desolate. Therefore the inhabitants of the earth are burned, and few men are left....The earth shall reel to and fro like a drunkard, and shall totter like a hut; its transgression shall be heavy upon it, and it will fall, and not rise again (Isaiah 24:5-6,20 NKJV).

We know that the whole creation has been groaning as in the pains of childbirth right up to the present time (Romans 8:22 NIV).

D. Times of crisis provide strategic prayer opportunities. When we take hold of our prayer assignments and pray in the Spirit, we are helping open portals to Heaven so that the King can find faith on the earth. We are standing in the gap that separates Him from the world He wants to save. We are serving as transmitters so that the language of Heaven can be heard on earth.

E. Storm warnings are being released. Times of shaking will become more severe as the endtimes unfold. God's Word and His character are like a measuring line; whatever does not match up with it will be shaken. God's warnings give people an opportunity to respond. Each storm requires a different response, but the responses have something in common—desperation.

1. Storms of God's judgment (Our response—a cry for mercy, requiring brokenness and tenaciousness)

2. Storms of dark demonic attack (Our response—authoritative intercession, requiring faith, endurance, boldness, and no common ground with the enemy)

3. Storms of the consequences of sins (Our response—repentance, requiring humility)

II. The Role of God's People in Times of Crisis

A. God governs (releases power to) the universe in partnership with His people through intercession. The majesty and mystery of intercession is seen first and foremost in Jesus' relationship with the Father.

    1. "He is also able to save to the uttermost those who come to God through Him, since He always lives to make intercession for them" (Heb. 7:25 NKJV).

    2. "Ask of Me, and I will give You the nations for Your inheritance, and the ends of the earth for Your possession" (Ps. 2:8 NKJV).

B. God has already determined the primary events in His eternal plan (Jesus' second coming, Jesus' reign over earth as King, the casting of satan into the lake of fire, the establishment of the New Heavens and New Earth, etc.). These events are non-negotiable. God will accomplish these things regardless of what people or demons do.

C. However, He has chosen to give His people a dynamic role in determining some of the measure of the "quality of life," both natural and spiritual. We can respond to the grace of God in prayer and meekness.

D. The place of prayer is the governmental center of the universe, or the way that God chooses to release His power. Prayer is transcendent, not limited by time or distance.

E. God opens doors of blessing and closes doors of oppression in response to our prayers. God reserves blessings until His people ask for them.

    1. "...You do not have because you do not ask" (James 4:2).

    2. "But this kind does not go out except by prayer and fasting" (Matt. 17:21).

    3. "Therefore the Lord longs to be gracious to you, and therefore He waits on high to have compassion on you....He will surely be gracious to you at the sound of your cry; when He hears it, He will answer you" (Isa. 30:18-19).

    4. "I sought for a man among them who would make a wall, and stand in the gap before Me on behalf of the land, that I should not destroy it; but I found no one" (Ezek. 22:30).

F. God has given the human race great dignity. We have been given free will, which means that we have the ability to make real choices that can cause good or evil results. If we choose righteousness, we have the power to open doors of blessings on others. When we live in rebellion, we open up legal entry points for demonic activity to be heightened in the earthly realm. Some of our choices now will affect us forever. This life is not a practice game.

G. Corporate intercessory worship is the primary means that God uses to release His government (power) in His relationship with Jesus and His redeemed. It is the highest expression of government in time and eternity. It is the most powerful weapon that exists.

H. "Trusting" the sovereign God to perform the role that He has actually assigned to us is non-biblical. We cannot do God's part, and He will not do our part. For example, God wants us all to be saved, but it does not happen because God will not violate our free will (see 2 Pet. 3:8-9).

I. We do not earn God's blessings by our prayers. Our prayers make it possible for us to more fully cooperate with Him in releasing blessings.

J. Many people who love prayer in the context of their communion with God do not yet have a revelation of the authority of intercession. Many worship leaders love Jesus and music, yet they do not have a revelation of the authority of corporate intercessory worship.

K. God's primary call to a nation in crisis is to gather in solemn assemblies. In other words, corporate intercessory worship and ambassadorial intercession are what we need most at such times.

Therefore also now, saith the Lord, turn ye even to me with all your heart, and with fasting, and with weeping, and with mourning: And rend your heart, and not your garments, and turn unto the Lord your God: for he is gracious and merciful, slow to anger, and of great kindness, and repenteth him of the evil. Who knoweth if he will return and repent, and leave a blessing behind him; even a meat offering and a drink offering unto the Lord your God? Blow the trumpet in Zion, sanctify a fast, call a solemn assembly: Gather the people... (Joel 2:12-17 KJV).

1. *Corporate* assumes a humble acceptance of differences in styles, doctrines, and personalities.

2. *Intercession* means to stand in the gap and to declare back to God biblical prayers and promises.

3. *Worship* includes prophetic music and singing, which unifies a body of people for sustained periods.

L. Corporate intercessory worship releases God's judgment:

Let the high praises of God be in their mouth, and a two-edged sword in their hand, to execute vengeance on the nations, and punishments on the peoples; to bind their kings with chains, and their nobles with fetters of iron; to execute on them the written judgment—this honor have all His saints (Psalm 149:6-9 NKJV).

III. Old Testament Examples of Crisis Intercession

A. Abraham's bartering: Abraham cried out in crisis intercession as he stood in the gap for the people of Sodom and Gomorrah (see Gen. 18).

B. Rachel's desperate cry: "Now when Rachel saw that she bore Jacob no children, Rachel envied her sister, and said to Jacob, 'Give me children, or else I die!'" (Gen. 30:1 NKJV).

C. Moses' intercessory acts:

1. As the army of Egypt drew closer to Israel, Moses cried out to the Lord, and He told him to strike the waters with his staff. (See Exodus 14.)

2. Moses cried to the Lord to change the bitter waters to sweet, and he acted prophetically by throwing a branch into the water. (See Exodus 15:25.) (See also Jeremiah 23:5; Isaiah 11:1.)

3. Aaron and Hur stood with Moses as intercessory helpers, asking God to intervene against the Amalekites. (See Exodus 17.)

4. Moses told Aaron to take a censor with fire from the altar, and Aaron took his stand between the dead and the living, so that the plague was stopped. (See Numbers 16:41-50.)

5. Exodus 32:11-14:

Moses sought the favor of the Lord his God. "O Lord," he said, "why should Your anger burn against Your people, whom You brought out of Egypt with great power and a mighty hand? Why should the Egyptians say, 'It was with evil intent that He brought them out, to kill them in the mountains and to wipe them off the face of the earth'? Turn from Your fierce anger; relent and do not bring disaster on Your people. Remember Your servants Abraham, Isaac and Israel, to whom You swore by Your own self: 'I will make your descendants as numerous as the stars in the sky and I will give your descendants all this land I promised them, and it will be their inheritance forever.'" Then the Lord relented and did not bring on His people the disaster He had threatened (NIV).

6.   Deuteronomy 9:18-19:

Once again I fell prostrate before the Lord for forty days and forty nights; I ate no bread and drank no water, because of all the sin you had committed, doing what was evil in the Lord's sight and so provoking Him to anger. I feared the anger and wrath of the Lord, for He was angry enough with you to destroy you. But again the Lord listened to me (NIV).

D.   Gideon's 300 men: The sons of Israel cried out to the Lord, and God raised up deliverers from the power of Midian. Gideon's 300 men were those who knelt on one knee (worshipful watchers). (See Judges 6–7.) Worship precedes petitioning.

E.   Hannah's cry for a son: Hannah's barrenness caused her to cry out in desperation. (See First Samuel 1.)

F.   David's victory over Goliath:

David fastened on his sword over the tunic and tried walking around, because he was not used to them. "I cannot go in these," he said to Saul, "because I am not used to them." So he took them off. Then he took his staff in his hand, chose five smooth stones from the stream, put them in the pouch of his shepherd's bag and, with his sling in his hand, approached the Philistine (1 Samuel 17:39-40 NIV).

1.   David's prophetic act of intercession was to walk in his own armor and anointing, not in someone else's armor and anointing.

2.   As the taunts of the enemy came, David took five smooth stones (a tried and tested weapon) to assault Goliath.

G.   Elijah's travail: Elijah interceded with travail on Mount Carmel, asking God to send rain after three years of drought. (See First Kings 18:4-46. See also my book, *The Prophetic Intercessor*.)

H.   Elisha's prophetic actions and crisis intervention: (To learn more about this subject, refer to the lesson, "Prophetic Gestures and Actions" in my study guide, *Understanding Supernatural Encounters*.)

1. Elisha lay on the Shunammite boy and restored him to life. (See Second Kings 4:8-37.)

2. Elisha prayed and received revelation from God to throw flour into the pot of poisonous stew. (See Second Kings 4:38-41.)

3. Elisha prayed that his servant's eyes would be opened, and the servant saw the mountain full of horses and chariots of fire. (See Second Kings 6:17.)

4. Elisha prophesied over King Joash, telling him to take an arrow and shoot it out the window—the Lord's arrow of victory over Syria. (See Second Kings 13:15-19.)

I. Nehemiah's burden for restoration: Nehemiah was the king's cupbearer. (In a sense, we are all to be cupbearers to the King, offering ourselves to Him in service.) Nehemiah carried a desperate plea of forgiveness for the sins of his people and a prophetic burden for the re-establishment of Jerusalem.

Let Your ear be attentive and Your eyes open to hear the prayer Your servant is praying before You day and night for Your servants, the people of Israel. I confess the sins we Israelites, including myself and my father's house, have committed against You. We have acted very wickedly toward You. We have not obeyed the commands, decrees and laws You gave Your servant Moses (Nehemiah 1:6-7 NIV).

The king said to me, "What is it you want?" Then I prayed to the God of heaven, and I answered the king, "If it pleases the king and if your servant has found favor in his sight, let him send me to the city in Judah where my fathers are buried so that I can rebuild it" (Nehemiah 2:4-5 NIV).

J. Esther's divine appointment: Esther was raised up to stand in the gap in a time of crisis that could have resulted in the genocide of the entire Jewish people. (See the entire Book of Esther.)

K. Isaiah's persistent petitioning: True revival comes forth when God's people let their inner beings be filled with the pain, suffering, agony, and oppression of the people, and with the response of God's heart. It causes them to cry out as a woman in travail, as Isaiah did. Isaiah "lived in the *until* clauses," praying in persistent faith during the gaps between the revelation and the fulfillment:

For Zion's sake I will not hold My peace, and for Jerusalem's sake I will not rest, **until** *her righteousness goes forth as brightness, and her salvation as a lamp that* *burns. The Gentiles shall see your righteousness, and all kings your glory. You shall be called by a new name, which the mouth of the Lord will name (Isaiah 62:1-2 NKJV).*

*On your walls, O Jerusalem, I have appointed watchmen; all day and all night they will never keep silent. You who remind the Lord, take no rest for yourselves; and give Him no rest **until** He establishes and makes Jerusalem a praise in the earth (Isaiah 62:6-7).*

L. Jeremiah's warnings and pleas: Of Josiah, Jeremiah prophesied, "'He pled the cause of the afflicted and needy; then it was well. Is not that what it means to know Me?' declares the Lord" (Jer. 22:16 NASB). Crying out to God for intervention is a doorway into knowing God's mercy, getting close to His heart, feeling His burdens, and carrying His burning desire for justice.

M. Daniel's model of character and authority: Not caring whether his actions resulted in a death sentence, Daniel maintained his prayer life before God. He also pled for the fulfillment of former prophecies about God's people, with whom he was in exile in Babylon. He picked up the baton that had been given to the previous generation 70 years earlier, not resting in the assumption that God would simply act to fulfill His word now that the time was completed. Instead, he confessed generational sins in order to remove the blockages to the completion of God's promises. His consistency, his faith, his humility, and his obedience to God remain one of the finest examples of godly character in the Bible. And his prayers were answered as He reminded God of His Word.

N. Joel's trumpet sound: The prophet Joel didn't know that his call would echo through the centuries to the present day. His call to pray, fast, weep, and travail has been used in the past and will be used again to change times of desolation into times of restoration through holy consecration. (See Joel 1:13-14.)

O. Amos—holding off judgment: The prophet Amos interceded when he received visionary revelations, and his prayers are perhaps the premiere examples of prophetic crisis intercession in the Bible. Wherever the judgment of God had been pronounced, Amos set himself to interceding until the Lord relented and His hand of judgment was lifted. Whether it was judgment by locusts, judgment by fire, or judgment by plumb line, Amos said to the Lord, "Sovereign Lord, forgive! How can Jacob survive? He is so small!" And every time, incredibly, "the Lord relented. 'This will not happen,' the Lord said" (Amos 7:1-9 NIV).

1.   Like Amos, we need to be those who will hold off wars, volcanic eruptions, earthquakes, and natural calamities by calling for the mercy of God to be released.

2.   We must also realize that the judgment of God can be His mercy. We need discernment in these matters.

IV. New Testament Examples of Crisis Intercession

A. Jesus Christ our Lord: One example of Jesus' crisis intercession is the calming of the storm (see Matt. 8:23-27). The storm was so violent that the boat was about to sink. Jesus spoke to the storm and rebuked it, and immediately the wind and the waves died down. The disciples were astonished, saying, "What kind of man is this? Even the winds and the waves obey Him!" (Matt. 8:27 NIV). Why don't we exercise the same level of apostolic authority today? If we did, Jesus would become a living reality to people.

B. The Church's fervent intercession:

1.   The early Church came under threats and persecution. As the people prayed fervently, they were all filled with the Holy Spirit and boldness, and the place where they were gathering was shaken. (See Acts 4:29-31.)

2.   Intense intercession from the local church resulted in an angel being released from Heaven to Peter's jail cell and his ultimate release. (See Acts 12:2-17.)

C. Paul's prayer and worship:

1.   Paul and Silas were in prison, and they prayed and praised the Lord. Suddenly, an earthquake came, and they were set free. This resulted in the conversion of the jailer and his entire household. (See Acts 16:22-33.)

2.   Paul requested from prison for prayers to be lifted up on his behalf so that he could proclaim the Gospel with boldness. (See Ephesians 6:18-20.)

Summary

God wants to anoint His watchmen today with the grace and authority for crisis intercession. He is looking for humble people who understand the times in which they live, who have learned the principles of intercession, confession, and repentance, and who have cultivated an authentic spirit of faith mingled with the spirit of revelation from the heart of the Father.

Reflection Questions

Lesson 4: Intercessory Prayer Storm in Times of Crisis

(Answers to these questions can be found in the back of the study guide.)

1. What does it mean to say that "the shaking and the glory come together"?

    _____

    _____

2. (Review I.E.) What are the three responses of the people of God to the three types of storms?

    a. Storms of God's judgment. Our response: _____

    b. Storms of dark demonic attack. Our response: _____

    c. Storms of consequences of sins. Our response: _____

3. In response to our prayers, God opens doors of _____ and closes doors of oppression.

4. Of the 15 examples of Old Testament intercession, select three that exemplify a type of prayer you would like to learn more about. Write down why you want to know more about these types of prayer.

    _____

    _____

    _____

5. Times of _____ provide strategic prayer opportunities.

PERSONAL APPLICATION QUESTION

6. Give an example of a time when your prayers were informed by "hearing the heart of the Father." (If you do not feel that this has ever happened for you, can you determine why?)

_____

_____

_____

_____

_____

_____

_____

Lesson 5

PRAYER WITH FASTING—GOD'S WAY

"Yet even now," declares the Lord, "Return to Me with all your heart, and with fasting, weeping and mourning; and rend your heart and not your garments." Now return to the Lord your God, for He is gracious and compassionate, slow to anger, abounding in lovingkindness and relenting of evil. Who knows whether He will not turn and relent and leave a blessing behind Him...? (Joel 2:12-14).

I. **Biblical Fasting**

   A. What does it mean to fast?

      1. Fasting is a deliberate act. Fasting means turning from food or other personal appetites so that we might focus our attention on God.

      2. Fasting is abstaining from food for spiritual purposes. Fasting is a sacrifice. Sacrifice releases power or a display of God's blessing.

      3. The purpose of fasting is to discipline the body and quiet the soul so that one can hear from God. Although the Scriptures show us that prayer and fasting are linked together, fasting doesn't buy us anything from God; rather, it aligns us with His purposes and will.

   B. Fasting in the Old Testament

      1. The life of Moses: The first mention of the discipline of fasting in Scripture is the 40-day fast of Moses when God met with him on Mount Sinai, where he received the directions for building the tabernacle and the Ten Commandments (see Exod. 34:28; Deut. 9:9). Moses did a second 40-day fast when the tablets of stone were replaced (see Deut. 9:18).

      2. Historical development: The verb *fasting* comes from the Hebrew term *tsum,* which refers to self-denial. The noun *tsum* means voluntary

abstinence from food.[1] Most scholars believe that the first fasting occurred as a loss of appetite during times of great distress.

a. Hannah was greatly distressed due to her barrenness, so she "wept and did not eat" (1 Sam. 1:7 NKJV).

b. King Ahab, when he failed to obtain Naboth's vineyard, lay down on his bed, turned his face to the wall, and "would eat no food" (1 Kings 21:4 NKJV).

c. David used fasting to express his grief at Abner's death. "When all the people came to persuade David to eat food while it was still day, David took an oath, saying, 'God do so to me, and more also, if I taste bread or anything else till the sun goes down'" (2 Sam. 3:35 NKJV).

3. The Day of Atonement: The only required yearly fast was on the Day of Atonement, when the High Priest would offer sacrifices for the sins of the people. The people fasted for self-examination and to demonstrate remorse.

Aaron shall bring the bull of the sin offering, which is for himself, and make atonement for himself and for his house, and shall kill the bull as the sin offering which is for himself.... Then he shall kill the goat of the sin offering, which is for the people, bring its blood inside the veil, do with that blood as he did with the blood of the bull, and sprinkle it on the mercy seat and before the mercy seat....Aaron shall lay both his hands on the head of the live goat, confess over it all the iniquities of the children of Israel, and all their transgressions, concerning all their sins, putting them on the head of the goat, and shall send it away into the wilderness by the hand of a suitable man.... This shall be a statute forever for you: In the seventh month, on the tenth day of the month, you shall afflict your souls, and do no work at all, whether a native of your own country or a stranger who dwells among you. For on that day the priest shall make atonement for you, to cleanse you, that you may be clean from all your sins before the Lord. It is a sabbath of solemn rest for you, and you shall afflict your souls. It is a statute forever (Leviticus 16:11, 15,21,29-31 NKJV).

a. Fasting releases God's presence. Fasting is a key to the supernatural.

b. Fasting aligns man with God's Word, God's will, and God's way.

4. An expression of grief and desperation: Fasting became a natural expression of human grief and a customary way to fend off the anger of God. Eventually, fasting became a way for making one's petition to God effective. As a national call, fasting was used to seek divine favor and protection or to circumvent the judgment of God. Therefore, it became a normal practice for a group of people to combine confession of sin, sorrow, and intercession with fasting.

C. Fasting in the New Testament

1. The Pharisees: Fasting was well-established within Jewish tradition by the time of Jesus. Unfortunately, it had become part of the "works" mindset of the established authorities, the Pharisees. It is believed that they fasted on Tuesdays and Thursdays.

   The Pharisee took his stand ostentatiously and began to pray thus before and with himself: God, I thank You that I am not like the rest of men—extortioners (robbers), swindlers [unrighteous in heart and life], adulterers—or even like this tax collector here. I fast twice a week; I give tithes of all that I gain (Luke 18:11-12 AMP).

2. John the Baptist and his disciples: John the Baptist was a Nazarite from birth (see Num. 6:2-8; Matt. 9:14-15; Luke 1:15-17). A Nazarite was "a person of the vow," and fasting was a regular part of his lifestyle. John's disciples followed his sacrificial lifestyle.

3. Jesus Christ: Jesus established an important contrast.

   a. He gave very few specific guidelines to His disciples concerning fasting. He did say that their fasting should be different from that of the Pharisees, namely, that it should be practiced to be seen by God and not to impress other people.

   Whenever you fast, do not put on a gloomy face as the hypocrites do, for they neglect their appearance so that they will be noticed by men when they are fasting. Truly I say to you, they have their reward in full. But you, when you fast, anoint your head and wash your face so that your fasting will not be noticed by men, but by your Father who is in secret; and your Father who sees what is done in secret will reward you (Matthew 6:16-18).

   b. Jesus also made a particular point of challenging John's Nazarite-influenced disciples with the new idea of what we now call the

Bridegroom fast (see Matt. 9:15), which promotes fasting *as an act of worship.* The response of those He came to save is to humble themselves, often with fasting, consecrating their whole lives to His service.

4. The early Church: The early Church practiced fasting, especially when ordaining elders or setting people apart for a special task.

    a. "While they were ministering to the Lord and fasting, the Holy Spirit said, 'Set apart for Me Barnabas and Saul for the work to which I have called them'" (Acts 13:2).

    b. Fasting was also practiced regularly by Paul and other Christian leaders.

But we commend ourselves in every way as [true] servants of God: through great endurance, in tribulation and suffering, in hardships and privations, in sore straits and calamities, in beatings, imprisonments, riots, labors, sleepless watching, hunger (2 Corinthians 6:4-5 AMP).

D. Accounts from Church history

1. Epiphanius, Bishop of Salamis (a.d. 315), wrote, "Who does not know that the fasts of the fourth and sixth days of the week [i.e., Wednesdays and Fridays] are observed by Christians throughout the world?"[2] (These days were chosen to prevent confusion with the Pharisees' Tuesday/Thursday fast days.)

2. Fasting before Easter: The early Church fasted for several days before Easter to prepare spiritually for the celebration of Jesus' resurrection. This turned into a 40-day time of partial fasting (Lent). In the second and third centuries, preparation for water baptism, which often occurred at Easter, included fasting.

3. Fasting in revival movements: All reformers up through the centuries practiced fasting. The founders of the monastic movements practiced fasting. Each of the 16th-century reformers practiced fasting, as did the leaders of the evangelical great awakenings. John Wesley would not ordain a man to ministry unless he practiced fasting two days a week. Jonathan Edwards fasted before he preached his now-famous sermon, "Sinners in the Hands of An Angry God." During the laymen's prayer revival in North America in the mid-1800s, Christians fasted in order

to attend lunch-hour prayer meetings. When Charles Finney felt that the Spirit's anointing had lifted, he would retreat and fast until it returned.

II. Nine Biblical Fasts[3]

A. The Disciples Fast: The disciples could not set a boy free from overpowering demonic control (see Matt. 17:14-21). In many translations, the account reads, "This kind [of spirit] does not go out except by prayer and fasting" (Matt. 17:21 NKJV). Jesus implied that the disciples might have been successful if they had fasted before they prayed. Modern disciples can employ fasting in order to "loose the bonds of wickedness" (Isa. 58:6), achieving victory over besetting sins and persistent, unhealed conditions.

B. The Ezra Fast: Ezra and the Jews returned to rebuild Jerusalem. As they journeyed, their enemies came against them. Ezra called a fast to pray for protection. (See Ezra 8:21-23.) We can call it an Ezra fast when we fast for solutions to problems, inviting God to overcome obstacles and furnish protection to that we can complete a task successfully.

C. The Samuel Fast: The ark of the Lord had been captured by the Philistines, and then it had been returned to Kiriath-jearim, where it had remained for 20 long years. When Samuel urged the people to reform their ways and to eliminate the sins that had allowed the ark to be captured and held, he and the people "gathered to Mizpah, and drew water and poured it out before the Lord, and fasted on that day and said there, 'We have sinned against the Lord...'" (1 Sam. 7:6). A "Samuel fast" represents a strong plea to God for revival of past glory and relief from sin, breaking off the kingdom of darkness so that the Kingdom of God can break in.

D. The Widow's Fast: Elijah went to the widow of Zarephath in the time of drought and famine. She was destitute, nearly starving, and preparing a final meal for herself and her son. Elijah's presence resulted in miraculous, sustained provision: "...She and he and her household ate for many days. The bin of flour was not used up, nor did the jar of oil run dry, according to the word of the Lord which He spoke by Elijah" (1 Kings 17:15-16 NKJV). In the same way today, we can present ourselves to the Lord in prayer and fasting, asking Him to relieve hunger.

E. The Elijah Fast: After Elijah prevailed over the prophets of Baal and ushered in the return of rain to the drought-stricken land, he had to run into the wilderness for his life. Jezebel wanted to kill him. All alone, he was desolate. God sent him an angel to feed him, and then Elijah ate nothing more for 40 days. (See First Kings 19:4,7-8.) Today we undertake an "Elijah fast" in order "to break every yoke" (Isa. 58:6) of emotional and mental anguish, in particular the aggressive religious spirit known as the "Jezebel spirit." Our desire is to ask God to control our lives and the lives of others, instead of allowing them to be controlled by emotional or mental problems.

F. The Saint Paul Fast: After he was struck blind on the road to Damascus, Paul went without food for three days, after which he was visited by the Christian Ananias, and both his eyesight and his vision of the future were restored (see Acts 9:17-19). His fast therefore becomes a model for us when we want to allow God's light to penetrate our blindness to bring us God's guidance as we make important decisions.

G. The Daniel Fast: Daniel and his three friends did not want to defile themselves with rich pagan foods in Babylon. Their steward allowed them to have only vegetables for their meals, after which they were remarkably healthier than their counterparts. (See Daniel 1:8,15.) The purpose of a Daniel fast today is to regain and maintain health or to obtain healing. "Is this not the fast that I have chosen?…Then…your healing shall spring forth speedily…" (Isa. 58:6,8 NKJV).

H. The Esther Fast: Esther and the Jews abstained from both food and water for three days in a desperate effort to stave off an enemy attack. The specific references to her fast and its results are found in the fourth and fifth chapters of the Book of Esther. When we undertake an Esther fast today, we are beseeching the Lord to protect us from the evil one (see Isa. 58:8).

I. The John the Baptist Fast: Because he came to announce Jesus' arrival, John the Baptist was Jesus' "forerunner." As a Nazarite from birth (see Luke 1:15), he was not allowed to drink wine or strong drink, which of course is a form of fasting. His disciples fasted also (see Matt. 9:14; Mark 2:18; Luke 5:33). To undertake a John the Baptist fast is to abstain from some degree of sustenance with the goal of obtaining favor for our testimony, influence, or witness before others. Inevitably, one of the results of such a fast will be to increase a person's holiness before God. The actual details of what the person abstains from are not as important as the goal of the fast.

III. Features of Fasting

A. Prayer: The primary activity that should accompany fasting is *prayer*. "Fasting and prayer" always go together.

1. "So we fasted and sought our God concerning this matter, and He listened to our entreaty" (Ezra 8:23).

2. "When I heard these words, I sat down and wept and mourned for days; and I was fasting and praying before the God of heaven" (Neh. 1:4).

3. "Yet when they were ill, I put on sackcloth and humbled myself with fasting. When my prayers returned to me unanswered" (Ps. 35:13).

4. "So I turned to the Lord God and pleaded with Him in prayer and petition, in fasting, and in sackcloth and ashes" (Dan. 9:3 NIV).

They said to him, "John's disciples often fast and pray, and so do the disciples of the Pharisees, but Yours go on eating and drinking." Jesus answered, "Can you make the guests of the bridegroom fast while He is with them? But the time will come when the bridegroom will be taken from them; in those days they will fast" (Luke 5:33-35 NIV).

B. Worship:

Now on the twenty-fourth day of this month the children of Israel were assembled with fasting, in sackcloth, and with dust on their heads. Then those of Israelite lineage separated themselves from all foreigners; and they stood and confessed their sins and the iniquities of their fathers. And they stood up in their place and read from the Book of the Law of the Lord their God for one-fourth of the day; and for another fourth they confessed and worshiped the Lord their God (Nehemiah 9:1-3 NKJV).

C. Confession of sin: "So they gathered together at Mizpah, drew water, and poured it out before the Lord. And they fasted that day, and said there, 'We have sinned against the Lord.' And Samuel judged the children of Israel at Mizpah" (1 Sam. 7:6 NKJV).

D. Fasting and humility go together. (See Deuteronomy 9:18; First Kings 21:27; Nehemiah 9:1; and Psalm 35:13; 69:10.)

E. Reading the Scriptures. (See Nehemiah 9:1-3; Jeremiah 36:6,10.)

F. Mourning and weeping: "And they mourned and wept and fasted until evening for Saul and for Jonathan his son, for the people of the Lord and for the house of Israel, because they had fallen by the sword" (2 Sam. 1:12 NKJV). (See also First Kings 21:27; Esther 4:3; Ezra 10:6; Nehemiah 1:4; Psalm 69:10; and Joel 2:12.)

G. Abstinence from sexual relations: "Do not deprive one another except with consent for a time, that you may give yourselves to fasting and prayer; and come together again so that Satan does not tempt you because of your lack of self-control" (1 Cor. 7:5 NKJV).

IV. **Different Types of Fasts**

A. Regular fast: abstaining from all food and drink, except water (see Matt. 4:2).

B. Partial fast: abstaining from a certain meal or restricting intake of certain foods.

C. Liquid fast: abstaining from all solid food for a determined period of time, while allowing liquid nourishment (broth, juice, water, etc.).

D. Absolute or complete fast: total restriction of all food and all liquid for a short period of time. (See Acts 9:9; Esther 4:16.)

V. **Contemporary Issues to Consider**

A. Fasting can include limitations on activities:

1. Athletic events (watching or playing sports, watching or undertaking other forms of recreation)

2. Entertainment (watching movies, videos, television, radio, video games, secular dancing, etc.)

3. Social functions (limiting outside engagements, conferences, seminars, even including normal Church activities, for short specific periods, to achieve times of purposeful isolation)

4. Reading (restricting reading of magazines, books, newspapers, other news media, and even Christian fiction)

5. Computers (restricting Internet access, games, e-mail, etc.)

B. Other forms of sacrifice that could be considered fasting:

1. Speech (phone calls, negative speech, criticism, amount of talking, limiting topics of conversation, vow of silence)

2. Dress (avoiding wearing certain types or styles of clothing)

3. Sleep (sacrificing sleep for the sake of prayer, such as in all-night prayer vigils, prayer watches at various hours, early morning prayer)

4. Work schedule (taking hours or days off from secular work or even ministry engagements to seek God's face)

5. Sexual relations (see 1 Cor. 7:5)

VI. The Vision of the Bridegroom Fast

A. In the last days: the book of Joel paints us a picture of the last days in which seeking God with fasting precedes the great latter-rain outpouring and a worldwide display of God's glory (see Joel 2:12,23,30-32).

B. Motivated by a lovesick heart: "Jesus said to them, 'Can the friends of the bridegroom mourn as long as the bridegroom is with them? But the days will come when the bridegroom will be taken away from them, and then they will fast'" (Matt. 9:15 NKJV).

C. The contemplative: a contemplative Christian fasts out of a lovesick heart. The motivation for a Bridegroom "fasted lifestyle" is passion for His presence, longing for His return, and brokenness as over a lover who has left.

D. From Arthur Wallis, *God's Chosen Fast*:

Before the Bridegroom left them He promised that He would come again to receive them to Himself. The Church still awaits the midnight cry, 'Behold, the Bridegroom! Come out to meet him' (Matt. 25.6). It is this age of the Church that is the period of the absent Bridegroom. It is this age of the Church to which our Master referred when He said, '"Then they will fast."'

These words of Jesus were prophetic. The first Christians fulfilled them, and so have many saintly men and women of succeeding generations. Where are those who fulfil them today? Alas, they are few and far between, the exception rather than the rule, to the great loss of the Church.

A new generation, however, is arising. There is concern in the hearts of many for the recovery of apostolic power. But how can we recover apostolic power while neglecting apostolic practice? How can we expect the power to flow if we do not prepare the channels? Fasting is a God-appointed means for the flowing of His grace and power that we can afford to neglect no longer.

The fast of this age is not merely an act of mourning for Christ's absence, but an act of preparation for His return. May those prophetic words, '"Then will they fast"', be finally fulfilled in this generation. It will be a fasting and praying Church that will hear the thrilling cry, 'Behold, the Bridegroom!' Tears shall then be wiped away, and the *fast* be followed by the *feast* at the marriage supper of the Lamb.[4]

E. The Global Bridegroom Fast: Mike Bickle (International House of Prayer, Kansas City) hosts a monthly Global Bridegroom Fast (GBF) on the first Monday, Tuesday, and Wednesday of each month. For more information, go to www.ihop.org/Group/Group.aspx?id=19844.

VII. Blessings Promised From Fasting With Prayer

A. Personal blessings: if you want to experience more of Jesus, start fasting with a focus on Him as the Bridegroom. Your fast—which is like God's *feast* for His Bride—will mature you so that you can enter into intimacy with your Bridegroom. You will be able to assume your true identity in Christ and be fully prepared for His return.

　　1. Receive more revelation of the beauty of our marvelous God as you pour over His Word.

　　2. Receive a greater measure of revelation in an accelerated way.

　　3. Experience an accelerated process of getting rid of hard-heartedness, old strongholds, and old mindsets.

　　4. Experience God's love for you and your love for Him as never before.

B. Isaiah 58:6-12 blessings:

Is this not the fast that I have chosen: to loose the bonds of wickedness, to undo the heavy burdens, to let the oppressed go free, and that you break every yoke? Is it not to share your bread with the hungry, and that you bring to your house the poor who are cast out; when you see the naked, that you cover him, and not hide yourself from your own flesh? Then your light shall break forth like the morning, your healing shall spring forth speedily, and your righteousness shall go before you; the glory of the Lord shall be your rear guard. Then you shall call, and the Lord will answer; you shall cry, and He will say, "Here I am."

If you take away the yoke from your midst, the pointing of the finger, and speaking wickedness, if you extend your soul to the hungry and satisfy the afflicted soul, then your light shall dawn in the darkness, and your darkness shall be as the noonday. The Lord will guide you continually, and satisfy your soul in drought, and strengthen your bones; you shall be like a watered garden, and like a spring of water, whose waters do not fail. Those from among you shall build the old waste places; you shall raise up the foundations of many generations; and you shall be called the Repairer of the Breach, the Restorer of Streets to Dwell In (NKJV).

1. Loosing the bands of wickedness

2. Undoing heavy burdens

3. Setting the oppressed free

4. Breaking the yoke of bondage

5. Attaining health

6. Maintaining righteousness

7. Seeing the glory of the Lord

8. Receiving guidance from the Lord continually

9. Having one's soul satisfied, even in times of spiritual drought

10. Achieving fruitfulness and productivity

11. Enhancing the ministry of reconciliation

C. Fasting disciplines our bodies, subdues our flesh, and allows our spirits to be strengthened by God's grace and peace. "I discipline my body and bring it into subjection, lest, when I have preached to others, I myself should become disqualified" (1 Cor. 9:27 NKJV).

D. Fasting is a strong tool that gives believers God's power against the works of darkness. "This kind [of spirit] does not go out except by prayer and fasting" (Matt. 17:21).

E. In Antioch, fasting with prayer was received by the Lord as acceptable ministry to Him. (See Acts 13:1-3.)

Summary

We have learned to feast and pray.
Now it is time to learn to fast and pray.[5]

Reflection Questions

Lesson 5: Prayer With Fasting—God's Way

(Answers to these questions can be found in the back of the study guide.)

1. Fasting means turning from _____ or other personal appetites so that we might focus our attention on God.

2. Fasting _____ man with God's Word, God's will, and God's way. (See I.B.3.b.)

3. Name and describe several of the nine biblical fasts described in the study guide.

    _____

    _____

    _____

    _____

    _____

4. "Fasting and _____" *always* go together.

5. In your own words, what is the Bridegroom Fast?

    _____

    _____

PERSONAL APPLICATION QUESTION

6. If you have fasted, what kind of fasting have you practiced the most? Describe what has resulted from your fasting, if possible.

_____

_____

_____

_____

_____

_____

Lesson 6

SOAKING IN HIS PRESENCE

Come to Me, all who are weary and heavy-laden, and I will give you rest. Take My yoke upon you and learn from Me, for I am gentle and humble in heart, and you will find rest for your souls. For My yoke is easy and My burden is light. (Matthew 11:28-30).

I. Come, Be With Me a While

A. Get oil for your lamp.

Then the kingdom of heaven shall be likened to ten virgins who took their lamps and went out to meet the bridegroom. Now five of them were wise, and five were foolish. Those who were foolish took their lamps and took no oil with them, but the wise took oil in their vessels with their lamps. But while the bridegroom was delayed, they all slumbered and slept.

And at midnight a cry was heard: "Behold, the bridegroom is coming; go out to meet Him!" Then all those virgins arose and trimmed their lamps. And the foolish said to the wise, "Give us some of your oil, for our lamps are going out." But the wise answered, saying, "No, lest there should not be enough for us and you; but go rather to those who sell, and buy for yourselves." And while they went to buy, the bridegroom came, and those who were ready went in with Him to the wedding; and the door was shut.

Afterward the other virgins came also, saying, "Lord, Lord, open to us!" But He answered and said, "Assuredly, I say to you, I do not know you." Watch therefore, for you know neither the day nor the hour in which the Son of Man is coming (Matthew 25:1-13 NKJV).

1. The ten virgins are all born-again believers. "I have betrothed you to one husband, that I may present you as a chaste virgin to Christ"

(2 Cor. 11:2 NKJV). Please note that the foolish virgins are not the same as the wicked, lazy, fearful, and cursed people that are portrayed in Matthew 25:25-26,41.

2. Each of them had lamps or ministries that brought light to others. Five were wise and prepared, but five were foolish and unprepared to go out to encounter Jesus as the Bridegroom. (See Isaiah 62:1; Zechariah 4:2; Matthew 5:15; John 5:35; and Revelation 1:20; 2:5; 11:3-6.)

3. The oil speaks of our relationship with the Holy Spirit. The oil of the Holy Spirit tenderizes and sensitizes our hearts to feel more of God's love for us. This increases our spiritual capacity for Jesus and our revelation of Him as it empowers us with zeal for righteousness.

4. At the midnight hour of history, the Spirit will raise up forerunners who cry out that Jesus is coming and that we must go out to meet Him (see Matt. 25:5-6).

5. The foolish virgins recognized the mistake of their neglect. "I counsel you to buy from Me gold refined in the fire, that you may be rich; and white garments, that you may be clothed..." (Rev. 3:18 NKJV). Spiritual preparedness is not transferable. Intimacy with Jesus cannot be gained by impartation. We must engage in the God-ordained process of acquiring oil for ourselves.

6. Many will miss out on future opportunities to be used in their fullest capacity. The Lord did not know or recognize them as those who were engaged to Him as the Bridegroom God (see Matt. 25:12).

B. Don't neglect your personal, devotional intimacy with Jesus. As Rick Joyner has often said, "You're as close to God as you want to be."

C. Jesus said, "Come unto me..." (see Matt. 11:28-30). When we come to Him, we receive rest for our souls. A divine exchange transpires as He takes our heavy load and gives us His grace. If we cover our devotional needs first, then we will have the grace of an empowered life to conduct our ministry of intercession and other missions.

D. Intercession is hard work without the grace of God. In fact, without the pervasive, soaking oil of the presence of Jesus' Spirit, prayer and intercession will shut down.

II. The Oil Is for Watching

A. Jesus' primary emphasis was on the importance of "watching" or developing a deep inner life in connection with the Holy Spirit (see Matt. 24–25).

But of that day and hour no one knows, not even the angels in heaven, nor the Son, but only the Father. Take heed, watch and pray; for you do not know when the time is…. Watch therefore, for you do not know when the master of the house is coming—in the evening, at midnight, at the crowing of the rooster, or in the morning—lest, coming suddenly, he find you sleeping. And what I say to you, I say to all: Watch! (Mark 13:32-33;35-37 NKJV).

Watch therefore, for you do not know what hour your Lord is coming. But know this, that if the master of the house had known what hour the thief would come, he would have watched and not allowed his house to be broken into (Matthew 24:42-43 NKJV).

Then He returned to His disciples and found them sleeping. "Could you men not keep watch with Me for one hour?" He asked Peter (Matthew 26:40 NIV).

B. Watchfulness establishes a lifestyle of encountering Jesus. Watching in the Spirit is essential in hindering satan from stealing our inheritance. Our primary inheritance is our heart connection with Jesus. Satan seeks to steal this aspect of our inheritance, knowing that by doing this he will also be able to gain access to our ministry inheritance.

1. "The thief does not come except to steal, and to kill, and to destroy. I have come that they may have life, and that they may have it more abundantly" (John 10:10 NKJV).

2. "Watch out that you are not deceived. For many will come in My name, claiming, 'I am He,' and, 'The time is near.' Do not follow them" (Luke 21:8 NIV).

C. What are we watching for? We are watching for the second coming of our Bridegroom, Jesus. If we are unprepared, we will be unable to greet Him.

But as the days of Noah were, so also will the coming of the Son of Man be. For as in the days before the flood, they were eating and drinking, marrying and giving in marriage, until the day that Noah entered the ark, and did not know until the flood came and took them all away, so also will the coming of the Son of Man be. Then two men will be in the field: one will be taken and the other left. Two women will be grinding at the mill: one will be taken and the other left (Matthew 24:37-41 NKJV).

III. The Remedy—The Oil of Intimacy and Soaking Presence

A. Fall in love with God all over again. You can experience personal revival by renewing your love relationship with Jesus. You can be changed, not just stirred, by returning to your first love. When you seek Him, you will find Him. You will find Him in the love letters He wrote to you (the Bible). You will find Him in the flowers that bloom and the creation that groans. You will find Him as you worship to the quiet music of a CD. You will find Him in the Body of Christ. Get alone with God the Father, God the Son, and God the Holy Spirit. Worship. Listen. Respond.

   1. Get still. Sit before Him in order to commune with Him. Take a "selah" pause. (See Second Samuel 7:18; Psalm 46:10; Habakkuk 2:20; and Revelation 3:20.)

   2. Draw near to His heart. (See Psalm 42:1-2; 65:4; 73:28; 84:1-4,10; Isaiah 55:1-3,6; James 4:8; and Hebrews 10:22.)

   3. Seek His face, not His intervention. Seek God for God's sake. (See Psalm 27:4,8; 63:1-8; Jeremiah 29:11-14; Matthew 7:7-8; and Hebrews 11:6.)

   4. Spend time in His presence. (See Exodus 33:14-15; Psalm 16:11; 89:15; Isaiah 29:13; 63:9; Lamentations 2:19; and Jude 24-25.)

   5. Get to know God. Encounter Him through His names and His Word. (See Jeremiah 9:23-24; Matthew 11:29; and Philippians 3:8,10.)

   6. Count all things as loss compared to knowing Him. (See First Chronicles 21:23; Second Samuel 24:24; Philippians 3:7-8.)

   7. Be overwhelmed with the amazing Person to whom you are speaking and who is speaking back. (See Exodus 15:3; Psalm 143:8,10; Isaiah 54:10; Lamentations 3:22-25; John 17:23b; Romans 5:5; 8:35-39.)

B.   Like Samuel, rest near the ark of His presence.

Now the boy Samuel was ministering to the Lord before Eli. And word from the Lord was rare in those days, visions were infrequent. It happened at that time as Eli was lying down in his place (now his eyesight had begun to grow dim and he could not see well), and the lamp of God had not yet gone out, and Samuel was lying down in the temple of the Lord where the ark of God was, that the Lord called Samuel; and he said, "Here I am." Then he ran to Eli and said, "Here I am, for you called me." But he said, "I did not call, lie down again." So he went and lay down. The Lord called yet again, "Samuel!" So Samuel arose and went to Eli and said, "Here I am, for you called me." But he answered, "I did not call, my son, lie down again" (1 Samuel 3:1-6).

1.   Samuel's bed was near the ark of the presence of God.

2.   He was told by Eli the priest to go and lie down again [by the ark]. This activity was repeated until Samuel learned to hear and discern the voice of the Lord and to respond accordingly.

3.   The voice of the Lord is released in the place of His presence.

Summary

Sit, rest, sleep right at His feet. Gather strength from being in His presence. Let the oil of His presence fill your lamp, so that you will be able to watch for Him. You will be no more effective as an intercessor in Prayer Storm than you are in your private "watching and waiting" times with the Lord.

Reflection Questions

Lesson 6: Soaking in His Presence

(Answers to these questions can be found in the back of the study guide.)

1. The oil speaks of our _____ with the Holy Spirit. (See I.A.3.)

2. How are we like the virgins?

    _____

    _____

    _____

3. What does it mean to "watch" like one of the virgins?

    _____

    _____

    _____

4. Samuel's bed was near the ark of the _____ of God.

PERSONAL APPLICATION QUESTION

5. The voice of the Lord is released in the place of His presence. Where, for you, is the "place of His presence"? What practical steps can you take to spend time in His presence?

_____

_____

_____

_____

_____

_____

_____

Lesson 7

TAPPING THE POWER OF HIGH PRAISE

Then Jonah prayed to the Lord his God from the fish's belly. And he said: "I cried out to the Lord because of my affliction, and He answered me....All Your billows and Your waves passed over me. Then I said, 'I have been cast out of Your sight; yet I will look again toward Your holy temple.' The waters surrounded me, even to my soul; the deep closed around me; weeds were wrapped around my head....When my soul fainted within me, I remembered the Lord; and my prayer went up to You, into Your holy temple....I will sacrifice to You with the voice of thanksgiving; I will pay what I have vowed. Salvation is of the Lord" (Jonah 2:1,3-5,7,9 NKJV).

I. **Born to be Instruments of Praise**

A. Praise is the place of God's residence. God is holy and cannot dwell in an unholy place. Praise sanctifies the atmosphere. "You are holy, enthroned in the praises of Israel" (Ps. 22:3 NKJV).

B. Praise is the way into God's presence.

1. "Enter His gates with thanksgiving, and His courts with praise; give thanks to Him and praise His name" (Ps. 100:4 NIV).

2. "You will call your walls Salvation and your gates Praise" (Isa. 60:18b NIV).

C. God's blessing releases praise.

1. God intervened in David's situation so that David praised the Lord.

I will extol You, O Lord, for You have lifted me up, and have not let my enemies rejoice over me....Sing praise to the Lord, you His godly ones, and give thanks to His holy name.... You have turned for me my mourning into dancing; You have loosed my sackcloth and girded me with gladness, that my soul may sing praise to

You and not be silent. O Lord my God, I will give thanks to You forever (Psalm 30:1,4,11-12).

2. The Hebrew phrase, *my glory* sometimes refers to the human tongue. "Therefore my heart is glad and my glory rejoices; my flesh also will dwell securely" (Ps. 16:9).

D. Praise is a garment of the Spirit. The gospel of praise can release us from the spirit of heaviness (replacing the dark, gloomy, and negative with the beautiful, glorious, and uplifting). Therefore, to some degree, our deliverance depends upon our obeying God's command to praise Him. (See Luke 4:18-19.)

The Spirit of the Lord God is upon me, because the Lord has anointed me To bring good news to the afflicted; He has sent me to bind up the brokenhearted, To proclaim liberty to captives and freedom to prisoners; to proclaim the favorable year of the Lord and the day of vengeance of our God; to comfort all who mourn, to grant those who mourn in Zion, giving them a garland instead of ashes, the oil of gladness instead of mourning, the mantle of praise instead of a spirit of fainting. So they will be called oaks of righteousness, the planting of the Lord, that He may be glorified (Isaiah 61:1-3).

E. Praise is a spiritual weapon.

1. As a means of deliverance

    a. When we begin to praise God in the midst of a terrible situation, salvation and deliverance enter in. (See Psalm 50:23.)

    b. When he was in the belly of the fish, Jonah began to offer praise, and God delivered him. (See Jonah 2:1-9.)

    c. In the middle of the night, praise opened the prison doors and loosed the bonds, setting Paul and Silas free. (See Acts 16:25-26.)

2. As a means of silencing the devil

    a. Because of our spiritual enemies, God has ordained praise that we might silence satan. (Whether for good or for evil, spiritual weapons are launched by people's mouths.) "Out of the mouth of babes and nursing infants You have ordained strength, because of

Your enemies, that You may silence the enemy and the avenger" (Ps. 8:2 NKJV).

    b.   Praise is a childlike expression of faith in a world where complicated minds tend to over-analyze circumstances and see no cause for such praise.

   3.   As the way into Christ's victory

    a.   God's intervention on behalf of His people is designed to bring forth praise and glory to His name (see Ps. 106:47).

    b.   Praise enables us to triumph with Christ (see Col. 2:15).

    c.   There is no time or place where the Church of Jesus cannot be victorious (see 2 Cor. 2:14).

F.   Praise is a sacrifice.

   1.   A sacrifice costs us something (see Jer. 33:11). We do not necessarily praise because we feel like it but because of what God has already done for us. Praise is the voice of the earthly Bride offering a "thank offering" to her heavenly Bridegroom.

   2.   Sacrifices can include more than the words of our lips. "Through Him then, let us continually offer up a sacrifice of praise to God, that is, the fruit of lips that give thanks to His name. And do not neglect doing good and sharing, for with such sacrifices God is pleased" (Heb. 13:15-16).

    a.   Praise (the fruit of our lips)

    b.   Doing good (the working out of the fruit of the Spirit)

    c.   Sharing (materials, goods, the fruit of our labor)

II. Praise, Worship, Thanksgiving

A. Praise

   1.   We praise God for who He is. Praise derives from God's greatness. "Great is the Lord, and greatly to be praised" (Ps. 48:1).

   2.   Praise is an utterance of the mouth that can be commanded.

B. Worship

1. Worship is primarily an inner attitude exhibited through the body. It is to bow down in submission.

2. Worship relates to God's holiness. Worship cannot be commanded. Consider the vision of worship in Heaven portrayed in Isaiah 6:1-4.

C. Thanksgiving

1. Thanksgiving is an utterance of the mouth. Thanksgiving relates to God's goodness. We thank God for what He does and has done.

2. Thanksgiving is directly commanded by God. In other words, giving thanks is related to being in God's will. Do you want to be in God's will? Just start thanking Him!

Rejoice always, pray without ceasing, in everything give thanks; for this is the will of God in Christ Jesus for you (1 Thessalonians 5:16-18 NKJV).

Let the peace of Christ rule in your hearts, to which indeed you were called in one body; and be thankful. Let the word of Christ richly dwell within you, with all wisdom teaching and admonishing one another with psalms and hymns and spiritual songs, singing with thankfulness in your hearts to God. Whatever you do in word or deed, do all in the name of the Lord Jesus, giving thanks through Him to God the Father (Colossians 3:15-17).

3. Thanksgiving is necessary to make other forms of prayer effective. It is like the "railroad track" that carries the payload of prayer. Paul urged the Philippians and the Colossians to "be anxious for nothing, but in everything by prayer and supplication with thanksgiving let your requests be made known to God" (Phil. 4:6) and to "devote yourselves to prayer, keeping alert in it with an attitude of thanksgiving" (Col. 4:2).

4. Thanksgiving, you see, is the key to releasing God's supernatural power. (See the story of the loaves and fishes in John 6:11,23 and the story of the raising of Lazarus in John 11:41-44.)

5. Thanksgiving and praise set a seal on the blessings that we have already received, keeping them safe. (See the story of the ten lepers in Luke 17:12-19.)

III. The When, How, and Who of Praise

A. When should we praise God?

    1. Every day, forever and ever, into eternity: "Every day I will bless You, and I will praise Your name forever and ever" (Ps. 145:2).

    2. At all times, continually: "I will bless the Lord at all times; His praise shall continually be in my mouth" (Ps. 34:1).

B. How should we praise the Lord?

    1. Praise God wholeheartedly, that is, with all of our hearts. "I will give thanks to the Lord with all my heart..." (Ps. 111:1).

    2. Praise God with understanding—and with skill. "...Sing praises with understanding" (Ps. 47:7 NKJV). "...Sing praises with a skillful psalm" (Ps. 47:7).

    3. Praise Him with lifted hands, a joyful mouth, and lips.

        a. "My lips will praise You. So I will bless You as long as I live; I will lift up my hands in Your name. My soul is satisfied as with marrow and fatness, and my mouth offers praises with joyful lips" (Ps. 63:3b-5).

        b. Lifting our hands is the only physical expression of praise that we are enjoined to use. "Therefore, I want the men in every place to pray, lifting up holy hands..." (1 Tim. 2:8).

    4. Dancing is used as a way to show gratitude, praise, and worship to God (see Ps. 149:3; 150:4).

    5. Our prayers go up to the nostrils of God like incense, and our uplifted hands are like the evening sacrifice (see Ps. 141:2).

C. Who should praise the Lord?

    1. Everything that has breath: "Let everything that has breath praise the Lord. Praise the Lord!" (Ps. 150:6 NKJV).

    2. At least 7 things in Heaven and 23 things on earth are called to praise God: angels, heavenly hosts, sun, moon, stars, heavens, waters above the

heavens, sea creatures, ocean depths, lightning, hail, snow, clouds, wind, mountains, hills, fruit trees, other trees, large animals, small animals, insects, birds, kings, peoples, princes, judges, men, women, old people, and young people (see Ps. 148:2-12.)

D. Who cannot praise the Lord? Only the dead cannot praise the Lord. "The dead do not praise the Lord, nor do any who go down into silence" (Ps. 115:17).

Summary

It is "the high praises of God in our mouths" that empowers us to the maximum. Through praise and worship, we enforce and extend the victory already won at Calvary. This is the honor given to all His godly ones (see Ps. 149).

Reflection Questions

Lesson 7: Tapping the Power of High Praise

(Answers to these questions can be found in the back of the study guide.)

1. Praise is the place of _____ residence. Praise is the way into _____ presence.

2. What are three ways in which praise is a spiritual weapon? (See I.E.)

   a. _____

   b _____

   c _____

3. What does it mean to say "praise is a sacrifice"?

   _____

   _____

   _____

4. "Be anxious for nothing, but in everything by prayer and supplication with _____ let your requests be made known to God" (Phil. 4:6).

5. Who cannot praise the Lord?

   _____

   _____

Personal application question

6. Write down a personal situation that seems intractable. Begin to praise God, worship Him, and thank Him now for this situation and for all that He intends to accomplish through it.

    _____

    _____

    _____

    _____

    _____

    _____

Part III

Patterns for a Prayer Storm

PRAYER FOR REVIVAL IN THE CHURCH

I will heal their backsliding, I will love them freely: for mine anger is turned away from him. I will be as the dew unto Israel: he shall grow as the lily, and cast forth his roots as Lebanon. His branches shall spread, and his beauty shall be as the olive tree, and his smell as Lebanon. They that dwell under his shadow shall return; they shall revive as the corn, and grow as the vine: the scent thereof shall be as the wine of Lebanon (Hosea 14:4-7 KJV).

I. **What Is Revival?**

A. Revival means to return to life or to recover from death or apparent death. Only something that was once alive can be revived. You can revive a drowned person, but what you're doing is bringing that person back to the life that he or she already had before they drowned. Revival is not the same as birth.

B. Revival means a return to activity after a season of lethargy, apathy, and languor. It's like a shock to the system. Emotions rise again as spirits are revived.

C. Revival is like a fire. What does fire do? Fire purifies, warms, empowers, and enlightens. Fire burns out impurities. Fire warms things up and even brings them to a boiling point. Fire is an energy source. When a fire is burning brightly, light is shed on the surrounding area. Spiritual fire purifies, warms, and enlightens. Revival fire warms up cold hearts and makes them want God again, and it releases zeal and power. Revival fire also releases revelation—the "lights come on."

D. Revival means recovery from oblivion or neglect or obscurity something that is a vital truth (i.e., the return to life of something that has been forgotten.) In spiritual revival, long-neglected truths are restored to life, and people rejoice to learn and obey them once again.

E. Revival makes people renew their interest in spiritual concerns. Their hearts and souls are restored with fresh life, and they are eager to engender more life wherever they go. Revival can be powerful enough to transform society.

F. Colin Dye said of revival:

Revival is a season of a powerful visitation from God. The term, properly speaking, belongs to the history of the Church subsequent to the New Testament era. However, during the historic revivals we can identify dominant elements that are also present in the New Testament Church. These center on God acting through powerful manifestations of His presence, strengthening the Church, and awakening the world. Indeed, there are many features of revival that flow out of the New Testament experience of God: conviction of sin, many conversions, powerful spiritual encounters, revelations of God, great assurance of salvation, spiritual fervor, and some kind of lasting legacy for the Church and society at large.[1]

G. In summary, revival involves a visitation from God in which His presence is powerfully and tangibly manifested in order to strengthen the Church and awaken the sleeping world to His reality. People in the midst of revival are convicted of sin, converted to the faith, impressed with God's truth, and propelled into firsthand experiences of a spiritual nature, and these experiences yield lasting results.

II. Scriptural Prayers for Revival

A. Psalm 85:1-6:

You showed favor to Your land, O Lord; You restored the fortunes of Jacob. You forgave the iniquity of Your people and covered all their sins. Selah. You set aside all Your wrath and turned from Your fierce anger. Restore us again, O God our Savior, and put away Your displeasure toward us. Will You be angry with us forever? Will You prolong Your anger through all generations? Will You not revive us again, that Your people may rejoice in You? (NIV).

B. Habakkuk 3:2: "Lord, I have heard of Your fame; I stand in awe of Your deeds, O Lord. Renew them in our day, in our time make them known; in wrath remember mercy" (NIV).

C. Isaiah 64:1-4:

Oh, that You would rend the heavens and come down, that the mountains might quake at Your presence—as fire kindles the brushwood, as fire causes water to boil—to make Your name known to Your adversaries, that the nations may tremble at Your presence! When You did awesome things which we did not expect, You came down, the mountains quaked at Your presence. For from days of old they have not heard or perceived by ear, nor has the eye seen a God besides You, who acts in behalf of the one who waits for Him.

III. The Role of Prayer in Spiritual Awakening

A. Scriptural prayers, such as the ones above, are like "prayer ammo." We can use them over and over.

B. In 1949, in the Hebrides Islands off Scotland, two elderly sisters, Christine and Peggy Smith, along with some young men, prayed fervently regarding revival, using Isaiah 64 as well as the following scriptural prayers:

For I will pour water upon him that is thirsty, and floods upon the dry ground: I will pour My spirit upon thy seed, and My blessing upon thine offspring: and they shall spring up as among the grass, as willows by the water courses (Isaiah 44:3-4 KJV).

Who shall ascend into the hill of the Lord? Or who shall stand in His holy place? He that hath clean hands, and a pure heart; who hath not lifted up His soul unto vanity, nor sworn deceitfully. He shall receive the blessing from the Lord, and righteousness from the God of his salvation. This is the generation of them that seek Him, that seek Thy face, O Jacob (Psalm 24:3-6 KJV).

Their fervent pleas were rewarded when God's Spirit fell on the islands to such a degree that spontaneous conversions occurred everywhere and the crime rate plummeted. It became one of the most phenomenal outpourings of the Holy Spirit since the Day of Pentecost. An evangelist named Duncan Campbell preached for many weeks and hundreds of people experienced life-changing "power encounters" with God.[2]

C. In 1976, Oxford-educated Church historian J. Edwin Orr gave a talk entitled, "The Role of Prayer in Spiritual Awakening" at the National Prayer

Congress in Dallas. A videotape of his presentation was made, and it is still available today. Here are some excerpts:

Dr. A.T. Pierson once said, "There has never been a spiritual awakening in any country or locality that did not begin in united prayer." Let me recount what God has done through concerted, united, sustained prayer.

Not many people realize that in the wake of the American Revolution there was a moral slump.... [Crime, drunkenness, profanity rose to alarming levels. Churches stopped growing and began to shrink.] Christians were so few on [the campuses of Ivy League colleges] in the 1790s that they met in secret, like a communist cell, and kept their minutes in code so that no one would know....The Chief of Justice of the United States, John Marshall, wrote to the Bishop of Virginia, James Madison, that the Church "was too far gone ever to be redeemed." Voltaire averred, and Tom Paine echoed, "Christianity will be forgotten in thirty years."

...How did the situation change? It came through a concert of prayer....In New England, there was a man of prayer named Isaac Backus, a Baptist pastor who in 1794, when conditions were at their worst, addressed an urgent plea for prayer for revival to pastors of every Christian denomination in the United States.

Churches knew that their backs were to the wall, so the Presbyterians of New York, New Jersey, and Pennsylvania adopted it for all their churches. Bishop Francis Asbury adopted it for all the Methodists. The Congregational and Baptist Associations, the Reformed and the Moravians all adopted the plan, until America...was interlaced with a network of prayer meetings, which set aside the first Monday of each month to pray.

It was not too long before the revival came. It broke out first of all in Connecticut, then spread to Massachusetts and all the seaboard states, in every case entirely without extravagance or outcry. [In the summer of 1800, when it reached Kentucky, which was a lawless territory at the time, it burst into wildfire. Great camp meetings were held, and pastors of every denominational affiliation assisted when as many as 11,000 people came to one communion service.]

Out of that second great awakening...came the whole modern missionary movement and its societies. Out of it came the abolition of slavery, popular education, Bible societies, Sunday schools and many social benefits....

[However, by the mid-1800s, conditions had deteriorated again.] In September 1857, a man of prayer, Jeremiah Lanphier, started a prayer meeting in the upper room of the Dutch Reformed Church consistory building in Manhattan. In response to his advertisement, only six people out of the population of a million showed up. But, the following week, there were fourteen, and then twenty-three, when it was decided to meet every day for prayer. By late winter, they were filling the Dutch Reformed Church, then the Methodist Church on John Street, then Trinity Episcopal Church on Broadway at Wall Street. In February and March of 1858, every church and public hall in downtown New York was filled. Horace Greeley, the famous editor, sent a reporter with horse and buggy racing around the prayer meetings to see how many men were praying: in one hour, he could get to only twelve meetings, but he counted 6100 men attending. Then a landslide of prayer began, which overflowed to the churches in the evenings. People began to be converted, ten thousand a week in New York City alone. The movement spread throughout New England, the church bells bringing people to prayer at eight in the morning, twelve noon, six in the evening. The revival raced up the Hudson and down the Mohawk, where the Baptists, for example, had so many people to baptize that they went down to the river, cut a big hole in the ice, and baptized them in the cold water: when Baptists do that they really are on fire....[Out of this revival came a young shoe salesman whose name became a household word, D.L. Moody.]...More than a million people were converted to God in one year out of a population of thirty million.

Then that same revival jumped the Atlantic appeared in Ulster, Scotland, Wales, then England, parts of Europe, South Africa and South India, anywhere there was an evangelical cause. It sent mission pioneers to many countries. Effects were felt for forty years. Having begun in a movement of prayer, it was sustained by a movement of prayer.

That movement lasted for a generation, but at the turn of the twentieth century, there was need of awakening again. A general movement of prayer began, with special prayer meetings at Moody Bible Institute; at Kenswick Convention in England; and places as far apart as Melbourne, Australia; Wonsan in Korea; and Nilgiri Hills of India. So all around the world believers were praying that there might be another great awakening in the twentieth century....

[Among the most notable results of this prayer is the well-known Welsh Revival of 1904] ...The movement went like a tidal wave over Wales. In five months there were a hundred thousand people converted throughout the country....It was the social impact that was astounding. For example, judges were presented with white gloves, not a case to try: no robberies, no burglaries, no rapes, no murders and no embezzlements, nothing....As the revival swept Wales, drunkenness was cut in half. There was a wave of bank-ruptcies, but they were nearly all for taverns. There was even a slowdown in the mines. You say, "How could a religious revival cause a strike?" It did not cause a strike, just a slowdown, for so many Welsh coal miners were con-verted and stopped using bad language that the horses that dragged the trucks in the mines could not understand what was being said to them, hence transportation slowed down for a while until they learned the lan-guage of Canaan. (When I first heard that story, I thought that it was a tall tale, but I can document it.) That revival also affected sexual moral stan-dards, I had discovered through the figures given by British government experts that, in Radnorshire and Merionethshire, the actual illegitimate birth rate had dropped 44% within a year of the beginning of the revival. That revival swept Britain. It so moved all of Norway that the Norwegian Parliament passed special legislation to permit laymen to conduct Com-munion because the clergy could not keep up with the number of the con-verts desiring to partake. It swept Sweden, Finland and Denmark, Germany, Canada from coast to coast, all of the United States, Australia, New Zealand, South Africa, East Africa, Central Africa, West Africa, touch-ing also Brazil, Mexico, and Chile....

As always, it began through a movement of prayer, with prayer meetings all over the United States as well as the other countries; and soon there came the great time of the harvest. So what is the lesson we can learn? It is a very simple one, as direct as the promises of God in Scripture: "If My people, who are called by My name, shall humble themselves and pray, and seek My face, and turn from their wicked ways, then I will hear from heaven and will forgive their sin and will heal their land" (2 Chron. 7:14 RSV).

What is involved in this? As God requires us to pray, we must not forget what was said by Jonathan Edwards: "...to promote explicit agreement and visible union of God's people in extraordinary prayer." What do we mean by extraordinary prayer? We share in ordinary prayer in regular worship services, before eating and the like. But when people are found getting up at six in the morning to pray, or having a half night of prayer until midnight, or giving up their lunchtime to pray at a noonday prayer meeting, that is extraordinary prayer. But it must be united and concerted.[3]

IV. Prerequisites for Revival

A. *Prayer* is an absolute prerequisite for revival. Prayer definitely changes things.

    1. Fervent prayer stems from a hunger and an intense desire for *change*. Something simply must change in the situation, because the situation is intolerable (see Matt. 5:6).

    2. If the situation is not intolerably terrible, it must change because it's boring. You may not quite be able to figure out what's wrong, but you are frustrated with the situation. At times like these, you can grumble and accuse—or you can pray.

B. *Networking* is another prerequisite for revival. People begin to pool their prayers and their efforts. They begin to cry out with one voice, "Lord, we need You! We are hungry for You. We are utterly dependent upon You." Praying in unity with others, as a team, gives feet to your restlessness and hope in the midst of your spiritual hunger.

V. What Revival Looks Like (Five Characteristics of True, Classic Revival)

A. An experiential conviction of sin: "...Unless I go away, the Counselor will not come to you; but if I go, I will send Him to you. When He comes, He will convict the world of guilt in regard to sin and righteousness and judgment" (John 16:7-8 NIV).

B. A passionate denunciation of sin: "You adulterous people, don't you know that friendship with the world is hatred toward God? Anyone who chooses to be a friend of the world becomes an enemy of God" (James 4:4 NIV).

C. A revelation of God's holiness: "It is written, 'You shall be holy, for I am holy'" (1 Pet. 1:16).

D. A deep awareness of God's love and mercy:

Who shall separate us from the love of Christ? Shall tribulation, or distress, or persecution, or famine, or nakedness, or peril, or sword? As it is written: "For Your sake we are killed all day long; we are accounted as sheep for the slaughter." Yet in all these things we are more than conquerors through Him who loved us. For I am persuaded that neither death nor life, nor angels nor principalities nor powers, nor things present nor things to come, nor height nor depth, nor any other created thing, shall be able to separate us from the love of God which is in Christ Jesus our Lord (Romans 8:35-39 NKJV).

E. A sometimes painfully heightened consciousness of eternity: Consider some of Jonathan Edwards' sermon titles during the revival in colonial America called the First Great Awakening: "Sinners in the Hands of an Angry God," "Wrath Upon the Wicked for the Uttermost," "Eternity of Hell's Torments."

And I saw the dead, the great and the small, standing before the throne, and books were opened; and another book was opened, which is the book of life; and the dead were judged from the things which were written in the books, according to their deeds. And the sea gave up the dead which were in it, and death and Hades gave up the dead which were in them; and they were judged, every one of them according to their deeds. Then death and Hades were thrown into the lake of fire. This is the second death, the lake of fire. And if anyone's name was not found written in the book of life, he was thrown into the lake of fire (Revelation 20:12-15).

VI. Responses to Revival

A. Prayer and more prayer is the appropriate response to desperate times. Extreme prayer at all hours of the day and night is the only appropriate application of effort before, during, and after a time of revival from God. God wants to revive His people, wherever they may live. In other words, revival is *His* work, and the way we participate is to engage *Him* in all prayerfulness.

1. Charles Finney, who was known for his phenomenal evangelistic successes during the Second Great Awakening in the United States, had equally phenomenal prayer support behind the scenes. He is quoted as having said, "Revival is no more a miracle than a crop of wheat. Revival comes from heaven when heroic souls enter the conflict determined to win or die—or if need be, to win and die."[4]

2. Matthew Henry, an English theologian and clergyman who composed the massive commentaries to the Old and New Testaments that bear

his name, wrote, "When God intends to do great mercy for his people, the first thing he does is to set them a-praying."[5]

3. Leonard Ravenhill, a 20th-century British revivalist, once said, "At God's counter there are no sale days, for the price for revival is ever the same—travail."[6]

4. E.M. Bounds, a Civil-War-era preacher and author who wrote prolifically about the importance of prayer, especially as it applies to all forms and stages of revival, wrote,

   The wrestling quality of importunate prayer does not spring from physical vehemence or fleshly energy. It is not an impulse of energy, nor mere earnestness of soul. It is an inwrought force, a faculty implanted and aroused by the Holy Spirit. Virtually, it is the intercession of the Holy Spirit in us.[7]

5. Prayer for revival is prayer for the Kingdom of God to come here and now. The only effective prayer is that which is inspired by the Holy Spirit Himself, and by definition, that prayer will be "violent," passionate, and untiringly persistent. "The kingdom of heaven suffers violence and the violent take it by force" (Matt. 11:12 NKJV).

B. Persecution, opposition, and challenge are the guaranteed responses to this kind of prayer. What you challenge will challenge you back. If you target individuals in prayer, persecution will come to you from individuals. If you target the Church in prayer, opposition will come from the Church. If you target the society around you, some segment of that society will fight back.

Summary

Like those who have gone before us, we need to press forward, undaunted, linked arm-in-arm and spirit-to-spirit with our fellow intercessors, walking together through the conflict until victory is achieved. And after revival has come, we need to support each other in the great work of stewarding the longed-for move of God.

Reflection Questions

Lesson 8: Prayer for Revival in the Church

(Answers to these questions can be found in the back of the study guide.)

1. See if you can define *revival* in your own words:

2. What are the two absolute prerequisites for revival?

    a _____

    b _____

3. What are the five characteristics of true, classic revival?

    a _____

    b _____

    c _____

    d _____

    e _____

4. When revival comes, what is the primary appropriate response to it?

    _____

5. What is the guaranteed response to this kind of focused prayer?

    _____

    _____

PERSONAL APPLICATION QUESTION

6. Which of the Scriptural prayers for revival catches the attention of your heart and spirit? Make that prayer your own fervent plea before Heaven. Find others who share the cry of your heart.

_____

_____

Lesson 9

PRAYER FOR ANOTHER GREAT AWAKENING—YOUTH

And it shall come to pass afterward that I will pour out My Spirit on all flesh; your sons and your daughters shall prophesy, your old men shall dream dreams, your young men shall see visions. And also on My menservants and on My maidservants I will pour out My Spirit in those days (Joel 2:28-29 NKJV).

I. **The Time Has Come for Another Great Awakening**

A. In 1967, a youth revival known as the Jesus Movement broke out, sweeping across the country, exploding on college campuses and in coffee houses.

B. The Catholic charismatic renewal, one of the largest movements in neo-pentecostal history, started the same year and ushered thousands of Catholics and Protestants into fresh encounters with Jesus, including the baptism in the Holy Spirit.

C. In 1967 also, Jerusalem was once again brought under the control of the Jewish people and the state of Israel. This marked the shifting of eras; the dispensation of the times of the Gentiles began to shift to the time when Jerusalem will become the last days' focus for God's activity in the earth.

D. All of this has significance for us today, more than 40 years later, because we need another great awakening, specifically a youth awakening, in order to see God's plan come to fruition.

II. **Revolution—Always Begins With Young Adults**

A. Revolutions always start on campuses. Almost every revolution—bad or good—has started with students on college and university campuses. From Marxism, Communism, and Nazism to the Moravians, the Azuza Street revival, and the Jesus People movement, every one has started with students or has had a great influence on students, who are hungry for change and willing to lay down their lives for a cause.

1. The campuses are where the future leaders are living and being trained.

2. More than 550,000 international students attend American universities, and 600,000 more attend foreign universities.[1]

3. Statistics show that more than 77 percent of all Christians make a decision for Christ before the age of 21.[2]

B. Campus ministry, Cambridge style: In 1799, an evangelical move of the Holy Spirit began at King's College, Cambridge, England. By 1877, students from across Cambridge's 17 colleges organized the Cambridge Inter-Collegiate Christian Union (CICCU), which in turn caused an increased interest in salvations and missions. An evangelistic campaign led by D.L. Moody and Ira Sankey resulted in a noticeable increase in enrollment in theology schools and involvement in missions, including the launching of the "Cambridge Seven" to China, led by C.T. Studd, who had been a well-known cricket player.[3] More than a century later, CICCU still exists and has helped with the formation of organizations such as InterVarsity, Campus Crusade for Christ, and the Navigators.[4]

C. The First and Second Great Awakenings: The First Great Awakening in North America and Europe was ignited by a Yale University graduate named Jonathan Edwards and by Oxford students John Wesley and George Whitefield. The Second Great Awakening was sparked by Timothy Dwight, the grandson of Jonathan Edwards, at Yale University. After his 1797 message to Yale students, nearly half of Yale's student body came to Christ in a few short months.

D. The "Haystack Five": Samuel Mills was a freshman at Williams College in Massachusetts in 1806, when he met with four friends for prayer about revival and world missions. When a rainstorm hit, they took refuge under a haystack and continued to pray (thus becoming known as the "Haystack Five"). "When the rain subsided, Mills stood up, slammed his fist into his hand, and announced, 'We can do this, if we will!' These five young collegians stepped out in faith and not only initiated the first nationwide student movement, but also began the first six mission agencies from North America.[5]

E. Student Volunteer Movement: In 1886, a 20-something young man named Luther Wishard, newly appointed leader in the YMCA, heard the story of the Haystack Five. Inspired by the story, he committed himself to a revival of the same vision and went on to found the Student Volunteer Movement, which became the largest missions movement of all time.

Over the next generation, students on every campus in the U.S. committed themselves to the "evangelization of the world in this generation." Over 20,000 of them sailed to the foreign mission field, and over 80,000 others had personally committed themselves to prayer and to financially support those being sent out.[6]

F. Evan Roberts and the Welsh Revival of 1904: At the age of 13, Evan Roberts began to seek the Lord. When he was 26, revival came to his hometown in Wales. He taught the people to pray two simple prayers, "Send the Spirit now for Jesus Christ's sake" and "Send the Spirit now more powerfully for Jesus Christ's sake." God's Spirit came so powerfully that 100,000 people were born again.

III. The Prophetic Promises of a Great Youth Awakening

A. Read your Bible with an eye toward young adults. You can see how readily God engages this generation for His purposes—even before colleges and universities existed. Biblical prophecies about the first and second comings of Christ are not confined to the prophetic books of the Old Testament. A surprising number are found in the Psalms.

The Lord says to my Lord: "Sit at My right hand until I make Your enemies a footstool for Your feet." The Lord will extend Your mighty scepter from Zion; You will rule in the midst of Your enemies. Your troops will be willing on Your day of battle. Arrayed in holy majesty, from the womb of the dawn You will receive the dew of Your youth [or Your young men will come to You like the dew] (Psalm 110:1-3 NIV).

This command I entrust to you, Timothy, my son, in accordance with the prophecies previously made concerning you, that by them you fight the good fight (1 Timothy 1:18).

B. When prophecy (biblical or personal) is neglected, the prayer movement is weakened. Prophetic utterances strengthen our resolve in prayer and obedience, providing significant focus.

    1. In 1975, the prophet Bob Jones had the first of a series of encounters with angels who spoke about an outpouring of the Spirit that would be characterized by prophetic intercession. In 1984, the Lord showed Bob that prophetic intercession would need to be joined by "compassion and worship" to be complete. The combination of these anointings would results in several things: revival in the Church, power evangelism in world missions, justice in society, pockets of mercy ("cities of refuge"), and worldwide intercession for Israel. Between 1975 and 1983, Bob was given over 100 prophetic revelations about a worldwide youth movement.

    2. In 1995, I had an intense dream and visionary experience in which I saw stadiums filled with young people praising God. I heard this piercing word, "The stadiums will be filled as out of the belly of the Promise Keepers movement shall come forth a Youth Extravaganza that will rock the nations." I'm expecting to see the fulfillment of this word.

IV. The Law of Night and Day Prayer

A. "And will not God bring about justice for His chosen ones, who cry out to Him day and night? Will He keep putting them off? I tell you, He will see that they get justice, and quickly..." (Luke 18:7-8 NIV).

B. Why should 24/7 prayer and worship arise today?

    1. 24/7 worship and prayer is done in Heaven and, therefore, should be done on earth.

    2. 24/7 worship and prayer releases God's justice on the earth.

    3. 24/7 worship and prayer fuels the Great Commission (see Matt. 28:19).

    4. 24/7 worship and prayer hinders the plans of the devil.

    5. 24/7 worship and prayer releases revival breakthrough.

    6.   24/7 worship and prayer prepares the way for Christ's second coming.[7]

C. The role of prayer in student revivals: In order to understand revival, we must understand the role of prayer in the history of revivals. J. Edwin Orr, the famous revival historian, said, "Young people in student-led prayer cells have been at the forefront in almost every awakening."[8] Even the Moravians have a share in this fact. (By the time Count Nicolas Ludwig von Zinzendorf had graduated from the equivalent of high school at the age of 16, he had started no fewer than seven different student prayer groups, and he continued his prayer disciplines while he was a student at the University of Wittenberg from 1716 to 1719.)

V. Maturity and Strength

A. We need to move in the spirit of Elijah, which means, we need to say, "God, give me a spiritual son or daughter." Young people in this "fatherless generation" need to look for spiritual parents who encourage them and intercede for them, helping them find their God-given passions and destinies.

B. Elders must bless young people with their time, knowledge, wisdom, strength, vision, and every good thing, treating them like full-grown plants and like "corner pillars," bestowing on them a high appraisal of their value and helping them to envision their future in the family of God. They must help them in practical ways by providing necessary resources and releasing authority to them to accomplish their God-given commissions. "Let our sons in their youth be as grown-up plants, and our daughters as corner pillars fashioned as for a palace" (Ps. 144:12).

Summary

*Moves of God always involve the younger
generation. Every one of us must pray
for awakening and renewal among young people.*

Reflection Questions

Lesson 9: Prayer for Another Great Awakening—Youth

(Answers to these questions can be found in the back of the study guide.)

1. In your own words, summarize why there is such a strong connection between revival and young people.

2. Using Bible software, a concordance, or a cross-referenced Bible, find another Old Testament prophecy that applies to young people. The references quoted in this study guide include Joel 2:28-29, Psalm 110:1-3, and Psalm 144:12.

3. _____ utterances strengthen our resolve in prayer and obedience, providing significant focus.

4. Name three of the six reasons that 24/7 prayer and worship is important.

    a _____

    b _____

    c _____

PERSONAL APPLICATION QUESTION

5. Do you know a young person to whom you can be a mentor in the spirit of Elijah? Write the name of that person down and begin to pray for opportunities to speak into his or her life. If you cannot think of anybody, begin to pray for opportunities. If you yourself are a young person, begin to pray for spiritual parents who can impart to you what you need.

   _____

   _____

Lesson 10

PRAYING YOUR FAMILY INTO THE KINGDOM

When He had stepped into the boat, the man who had been controlled by the unclean spirits kept begging Him that he might be with Him. But Jesus refused to permit him, but said to him, "Go home to your own [family and relatives and friends] and bring back word to them of how much the Lord has done for you, and [how He has] had sympathy for you and mercy on you" (Acts 5:18-19 AMP).

I. **God's Desires and His Ways**

    A. The Book of Revelation shows us God's heart.

        1. "They sung a new song, saying, Thou art worthy to take the book, and to open the seals thereof: for Thou wast slain, and hast redeemed us to God by Thy blood out of every kindred, and tongue, and people, and nation" (Rev. 5:9 KJV).

        2. "After these things I looked, and behold, a great multitude which no one could count, from every nation and all tribes and peoples and tongues, standing before the throne and before the Lamb, clothed in white robes, and palm branches were in their hands" (Rev. 7:9).

        3. A people of every nation: Before God's throne, there will be people of every nation (ethnic group), people, tongue, and kindred. Every *kindred* means every tribe and every clan.

        4. People of every family: Kindred, tribe, and clan refer to families. Before the throne of God, there will be people from every family.

    B. God wants to populate Heaven with people from every family, every tribe, and every clan on earth. He is the Father of them all.

For this reason [seeing the greatness of this plan by which you are built together in Christ], I bow my knees before the Father of our Lord Jesus Christ, for Whom every family in heaven and on earth is named [that Father from Whom all fatherhood takes its title and derives its name] (Ephesians 3:14-15 AMP).

C. Prayers precede conversions. "Owe no man any thing, but to love one another" (Rom. 13:8a KJV). Once I heard this statement from David Wilkerson, pastor and founder of Teen Challenge and Times Square Church, "Every man who is won in the street is first won in prayer." One of the ways that we pay our Romans 13:8 "love debt" is to commit our lives to praying others into the Kingdom of Heaven.

II. Price to Pay

A. It costs us something to make a way for someone else to come to Jesus. It requires a lot of love.

1. It causes pain.

2. It requires labor.

3. It takes time.

4. It requires much love.

5. It takes tenacity.

6. It requires holy desperation.

7. It often requires patience.

B. Biblical examples of the high cost of love include Mark 2:1-5 (the story of the paralytic who was lowered through a hole in the roof by his friends so that he could meet Jesus), Luke 7:1-10 (the story of the centurion who sought healing for his servant), and Mark 5:21-24;35-43 (the story of Jairus' daughter).

III. Our Priestly Role

A. Priesthood of believers: We are all called into the priesthood of believers. We have the responsibility, the privilege, and the authority to bring someone else into the presence of Christ.

You shall make a breastpiece of judgment, the work of a skillful workman; like the work of the ephod you shall make it: of gold, of blue and purple and scarlet material and fine twisted linen you shall make it. It shall be square and folded double, a span in length and a span in width. You shall mount on it four rows of stones; the first row shall be a row of ruby, topaz and emerald; and the second row a turquoise, a sapphire and a diamond; and the third row a jacinth, an agate and an amethyst; and the fourth row a beryl and an onyx and a jasper; they shall be set in gold filigree. The stones shall be according to the names of the sons of Israel: twelve, according to their names; they shall be like the engravings of a seal, each according to his name for the twelve tribes.... Aaron shall carry the names of the sons of Israel in the breastpiece of judgment over his heart when he enters the holy place, for a memorial before the Lord continually. You shall put in the breastpiece of judgment the Urim and the Thummim, and they shall be over Aaron's heart when he goes in before the Lord; and Aaron shall carry the judgment of the sons of Israel over his heart before the Lord continually (Exodus 28:15-21,29-30).

C. The priest's breastpiece was adorned with four rows of precious stones, each of which symbolized one of the 12 tribes of Israel. He carried them over his heart.

   1. Family representatives: We each have the place as a priest to carry "stones" upon our hearts. One of the places of our greatest authority is carrying our family members. In a priestly, intercessory manner, we represent our families.

   2. National and regional representatives: We have a certain priestly responsibility for the country that we live in, for our city, and for our neighborhood.

   3. Representatives of our heritage: We also stand as priests before God on behalf of the heritage and the people from which we come. (For example, I represent the nation of Germany before God, because my Goll heritage is German. I represent the English and the Scots because of my mother's Burns heritage.)

D. Household salvation: "They said, 'Believe in the Lord Jesus, and you will be saved, you and your household'" (Acts 16:31). God's heart is for "household salvations." Some of us, however, because of our hurt and pain, and because of not having a good relationship with our parents, have hardened our hearts in bitterness against our families. But God has given us this role. We need to exercise our responsibility to pray for the salvation of our family members so that they can come forth into the fullness of what He has destined for them to be and to do.

IV. **Practical Ways of Praying Your Family Into God's Family**

A. Ask God to soften their hearts. Pray for the condition of their hearts to change. "And I will give them one heart [a new heart] and I will put a new spirit within them; and I will take the stony [unnaturally hardened] heart out of their flesh, and will give them a heart of flesh [sensitive and responsive to the touch of their God]" (Ezek. 11:19 AMP).

B. Ask God to send a spirit of conviction. Ask for the release of the spirit of conviction of sin, righteousness, and judgment to come. "And He, when He comes, will convict the world concerning sin and righteousness and judgment" (John 16:8).

C. Ask God to send a spirit of revelation. Ask for the spirit of wisdom and revelation (dreams, visions, and angelic visitations).

[I pray] *that the God of our Lord Jesus Christ, the Father of glory, may give to you a spirit of wisdom and of revelation in the knowledge of Him. I pray that the eyes of your heart may be enlightened, so that you will know what is the hope of His calling, what are the riches of the glory of His inheritance in the saints, and what is the surpassing greatness of His power toward us who believe...* (Ephesians 1:17-19).

D. Ask God to bring His Word to their remembrance. Ask the Lord to bring to their remembrance any of the good words of God that they were taught from their childhood to this day.

1. "But the Helper, the Holy Spirit, whom the Father will send in My name, He will teach you all things, and bring to your remembrance all that I said to you" (John 14:26).

2. "So will My word be which goes forth from My mouth; it will not return to Me empty, without accomplishing what I desire, and without succeeding in the matter for which I sent it" (Isaiah 55:11).

E. Pray prayers of forgiveness. Forgive your mother, father, son, daughter. Forgiveness is the master key that unlocks the prison door to a heart of stone. Through forgiveness comes a place of identification. The model prayer of Jesus is not an individual prayer. It is a corporate prayer: "*Our* Father who is in heaven....Give *us* this day *our* daily bread....Forgive *us our* debts [sins]..." (see Matt. 6:9-15).

F. Pray for laborers for the harvest. This is a prayer that the Lord Jesus Himself recommended. "Ask the Lord of the harvest, therefore, to send out workers into His harvest field" (Matt. 9:38 NIV).

G. Pray for a revelation of eternity. In some ways, praying for a revelation of eternity is like praying for the release of a spirit of conviction. Here, however, you're asking the Lord to give a person an awareness of the realities of both Heaven and hell. Many people live their whole lives as if that's all there is. They need to have their eyes opened to the startling reality of an eternal Heaven and hell. They also need to recognize that no one is righteous enough to make it to Heaven without Jesus. You can combine this prayer with a prayer for revelation, asking even for dreams of Heaven and hell. You can combine it with a prayer for remembrance of something they once heard about Heaven or hell. People need a revelation of eternity before they will consider Jesus' invitation to join Him in Heaven.

H. Resist the enemy. Pray to break the powers of darkness that are generational and that are hindering your loved ones from the saving power of Jesus' blood. (See my study guide, *Deliverance from Darkness*, for more on this subject.)

I. Solicit other people's prayers. Enroll other intercessors to pray for your family.

1. "Pray on my behalf, that utterance may be given to me in the opening of my mouth, to make known with boldness the mystery of the gospel, for which I am an ambassador in chains; that in proclaiming it I may speak boldly, as I ought to speak" (Eph. 6:19-20).

2. "...He will yet deliver us, you also joining in helping us through your prayers, so that thanks may be given by many persons on our behalf for the favor bestowed on us through the prayers of many" (2 Cor. 1:10-11).

J.   Pray for a revelation of God's love. This may be the most important point. Ask God to overwhelm your family member(s) with His love. It's the kindness of God that draws us to repentance (see Rom. 2:4). Of course, He will use difficult circumstances to make someone desperate, but don't pray for Him to send difficulties. Don't partner with the devil's work. Partner with God, who is good all the time, and pray for a revelation of God's love in the midst of whatever happens. Otherwise, times of crisis will be wasted. If the person doesn't grasp the fact that God loves him or her right in the middle of a grave situation, the person may simply walk away, adjust to it, or otherwise not gain any eternal benefit from it.

Summary

We can release our faith and believe the Lord
for more of His presence to come to our families.
We stand as prophets, priests, and kings of our own
families before the Lord. We can let revival begin in our
own homes and families for the glory of God's great name.

Reflection Questions

Lesson 10: Praying Your Family Into the Kingdom

(Answers to these questions can be found in the back of the study guide.)

1. The desire of God's heart is to have people from every nation, people, tribe, tongue, and _____ in Heaven, worshipping before His throne.

2. In what ways does it cost us something to make a way for someone else to come to Jesus?

3. As priestly intercessors, each of us has particular authority and a responsibility to remember to pray for our _____, our nation/region, and our national heritage. (See III.C.)

4. "Believe in the Lord Jesus, and you will be saved, you and your _____" (Acts 16:31).

5. List at least five specific and practical ways that you can pray for your family.

    a _____

    b _____

    c _____

    d _____

    e _____

PERSONAL APPLICATION QUESTION

6. Can you identify the family member or members that you most need to carry in prayer right now? Write down the name(s) and find ways to remind yourself to pray more faithfully and effectively.

_____

_____

_____

Lesson 11

Praying for People in Authority

I urge that entreaties and prayers, petitions and thanksgivings, be made on behalf of all men, for kings and all who are in authority, so that we may lead a tranquil and quiet life in all godliness and dignity. This is good and acceptable in the sight of God our Savior, who desires all men to be saved and to come to the knowledge of the truth (1 Timothy 2:1-4).

I. **High Priority to God**

A. Prayers for people who are in positions of authority have a high priority in the heart of God. We see this in Scriptures such as First Timothy 2:1-4, which is an apostolic admonition for prayer.

1. When South African pastor and writer Andrew Murray read First Timothy 2:1-4, he wrote in response:

   What a faith in the power of prayer! A few feeble and despised Christians are to influence the mighty Roman emperors, and help in securing peace and quietness. Let us believe that prayer is a power that is taken up by God in His rule of the world. Let us pray for our country and its rulers, for all the rulers of the world, for rulers in cities or districts in which we are interested. When God's people unite in this, they may count upon their prayers effecting in the unseen world more than they know. Let faith hold this fast.[1]

2. Jack W. Hayford, founding pastor of The Church on the Way in Van Nuys, California, comments,

   You and I can help decide [whether]...blessing or cursing...happens on earth. We will determine whether God's goodness is released toward specific situations or whether the power of sin and Satan is permitted to prevail. Prayer is the determining factor.[2]

B. How to pray. Many other Scriptures help us understand how to pray for people who are in positions of authority.

1. "Honor all people. Love the brotherhood. Fear God. Honor the king" (1 Pet. 2:17 NKJV).

2. "Fear the Lord and the king, my son, and do not join with the rebellious, for those two will send sudden destruction upon them, and who knows what calamities they can bring?" (Prov. 24:21-22 NIV).

3. "When the righteous are in authority, the people rejoice; but when a wicked man rules, the people groan" (Prov. 29:2 NKJV).

4. Romans 13:1-7:

Every person is to be in subjection to the governing authorities For there is no authority except from God, and those which exist are established by God. Therefore whoever resists authority has opposed the ordinance of God; and they who have opposed will receive condemnation upon themselves. For rulers are not a cause of fear for good behavior, but for evil. Do you want to have no fear of authority? Do what is good and you will have praise from the same; for it is a minister of God to you for good. But if you do what is evil, be afraid; for it does not bear the sword for nothing; for it is a minister of God, an avenger who brings wrath on the one who practices evil. Therefore it is necessary to be in subjection, not only because of wrath, but also for conscience' sake. For because of this you also pay taxes, for rulers are servants of God, devoting themselves to this very thing. Render to all what is due them: tax to whom tax is due; custom to whom custom; fear to whom fear; honor to whom honor.

C. Why should we pray for those who are in authority?

1. Note two reasons in First Timothy 2:1-4:

    a. "So that we may lead a tranquil and quiet life in all godliness and dignity."

    b. So that God can save all men and bring them to a knowledge of the truth.

2. Without prayer, you will not have power to carry out your plans. As the late Derek Prince said, prayer-less intentions are like a building that is

wired for electricity, but if it's not connected to a power source, nothing will work, even if the wires are in good order and the light fixtures are beautiful.

3. We should pray for those who are in authority simply to be obedient to the will of God. He also wants us to obey, as far as it is possible to do so, people who are in authority. If you "do good," as Romans 13:1-7 says, you will have no need to be fearful of the authorities.

D. Who should you pray for?

1. From a United States government perspective, you should pray for the 16 individuals who make most of the key governmental decisions in the United States: our President, the nine justices of the Supreme Court, the two senators from your state, the U.S. congressperson from your district, the governor of your state, your state senator, your state representative, and also for others who work on those levels of government.

2. You should pray for spiritual leaders on all levels—from your local pastor and church staff members to regional leaders, national leaders, and anyone who oversees an aspect of spiritual life in the Church.

3. You should pray for marketplace leaders, for the "elders" who "sit at the gates" of your city, for those who drive the commerce where you live.[3]

4. You should pray, by name if possible, for people who oversee certain spheres and assignments.

E. What should you pray for?

1. For righteousness.

   a. "Righteousness exalts a nation, but sin is a disgrace to any people" (Prov. 14:34).

   b. "If a king judges the poor with truth, his throne will be established forever" (Prov. 29:14).

2. For the selection process. Some people in authority are selected by a vote. Many are appointed, or they grow into their role (job or career)

gradually. Pray that the wisest and best people will be selected for each job.

"Choose wise and discerning and experienced men from your tribes, and I will appoint them as your heads." You [the people] answered me [Moses] and said, "The thing which you have said to do is good." So I took the heads of your tribes, wise and experienced men, and appointed them heads over you, leaders of thousands and of hundreds, of fifties and of tens, and officers for your tribes (Deuteronomy 1:13-15).

    a.   In 1638, a colonial pastor named Thomas Hooker preached a sermon in Hartford, Connecticut based on Deuteronomy 1:13-15, and his sermon inspired the creation of the Fundamental Orders of Connecticut, the first written constitution in Western history, which created a government from which the government of the United States can trace its lineal descent. In his sermon, Hooker "forcefully asserted that the choice of public magistrates belongs to the people, that the privilege of election belongs to the people, and that those who have the power to appoint officers of government have the right to limit the power they hold."[4] Thomas Hooker's sermon concluded with the words, "As God hath spared our lives, and given us them in liberty, so to seek the guidance of God, and to choose in God and for God."[5]

    b.   Daniel Webster (1782–1852) wrote: "If we abide by the principles taught in the Bible, our country will go on prospering...but if we neglect its instructions and authority, no man can tell how sudden a catastrophe may overwhelm us and bury all of our glory in profound obscurity."[6]

3.   Ten ways to pray for people in authority.

    a.   Pray that they would realize their personal sinfulness and their daily need for the cleansing of their sin by Jesus Christ.

    b.   Pray that they would recognize their personal inadequacy to fulfill their tasks and that they would depend upon God for knowledge, wisdom, and the courage to do what is right.

c.   Pray that they would reject all counsel that violates spiritual principles, trusting God to prove them right.

d.   Pray that they would resist those who would pressure them to violate their conscience.

e.   Pray that they would reverse the trends of socialism and humanism in this nation, both of which deify man rather than God.

f.   Pray that they would be ready to sacrifice their personal ambitions and political careers for the sake of this nation, if yielding them would be in the best interest of their country.

g.   Pray that they would rely upon prayer and the Word of God as the source of their daily strength, wisdom, and courage.

h.   Pray that they would restore dignity, honor, trustworthiness, and righteousness to the offices they hold.

i.   Pray that they would remember to be good examples in their conduct to the fathers, mothers, sons, and daughters of this nation.

j.   Pray that they would be reminded daily that they are accountable to Almighty God for the decisions they make.[7]

4.   Use key Scriptures. Dick Eastman, the president of Every Home for Christ, suggests using three key Scriptures.

a.   Pray for leaders to have knowledge and understanding, which is more than mere information; it includes a grasp of history, roles, cultures and God's will. "When a country is rebellious, it has many rulers, but a man of understanding and knowledge maintains order" (Prov. 28:2 NIV).

b.   Pray that…

The Spirit of the Lord will rest on Him, the spirit of wisdom and of understanding, the spirit of counsel and strength, the spirit of knowledge and of the fear of the Lord. And He will delight in the fear of the Lord, and He will not judge by what His eyes see, nor make a decision by what His ears hear (Isaiah 11:2-3).

c. Pray that God will deal with tyrants, for the sake of His people. Pray that He will hedge in such leaders with limits and boundaries. "Because of your raging against Me, and because your arrogance has come up to My ears, therefore I will put My hook in your nose, and My bridle in your lips, and I will turn you back by the way which you came" (2 Kings 19:28).

d. Pray that leaders will govern honestly, humbly, and with mercy. "He has shown you, O man, what is good; and what does the Lord require of you but to do justly, to love mercy, and to walk humbly with your God?" (Mic. 6:8 NKJV).

II. **Resources for Praying for Those in Authority**

A. The National Day of Prayer (www.ndptf.org)

B. The National Governmental Prayer Alliance (www.nationalgpa.org)

C. Intercessors For America (www.ifapray.org) (See many links on the IFA Website, including America's National Prayer Committee, The U.S. Prayer Center, Mission America, and more.)

Summary

*While we each have special prayer assignments,
we are **all** called to pray for people who are in authority.
It is God's heart, His Word, and His command.*

Reflection Questions

Lesson 11: Praying for People in Authority

(Answers to these questions can be found in the back of the study guide.)

1. "I urge that entreaties and prayers, petitions and thanksgivings, be made on behalf of all men, for kings and all who are in_____, so that we may lead a tranquil and quiet life in all godliness and dignity. This is good and acceptable in the sight of God our Savior, who desires all men to be _____ and to come to the knowledge of the truth" (1 Tim. 2:1-4).

2. According to First Timothy 2:1-4, what are two good reasons to pray for people in authority?

    a _____

    b _____

3. We should pray for _____ in people who bear authority, because "Righteousness exalts a nation, but sin is a disgrace to any people" (Prov. 14:34).

4. List five of the ten recommended ways to pray for people in authority.

    a _____

    b _____

    c _____

    d _____

    e _____

PERSONAL APPLICATION QUESTIONS

5. Who are some of the individuals in authority over you (governmental, Church, employment, marketplace authorities)? List some names.

_____

_____

_____

_____

6. Create a Scripture-based prayer for a particular authority figure that you want to pray for.

_____

_____

_____

_____

Lesson 12

PRAYING EFFECTIVELY FOR ISRAEL

Sing with gladness for Jacob, and shout among the chief of the nations; proclaim, give praise, and say, "O Lord, save Your people, the remnant of Israel" (Jeremiah 31:7 NKJV).

I. **Fervent, *Effective* Prayer**

    A. "...The effectual fervent prayer of a righteous man availeth much" (James 5:16 KJV).

        1. The word *effectual* (or *effective*) is *energeo* in the Greek, meaning something that has worked in you and is therefore more effective.[1]

        2. Effective prayer is not dutiful or rote repetition, but rather, it taps into God's heart.

    B. Pray for the return to the land. *Aliyah* means the "ascent" or the "return to the land."[2] From 1989-2007, 1.3 million Jews made *aliyah* from the land of the north (the former Soviet Union). In 1991, 14,500 Ethiopian Jews made *aliyah*, practically overnight.[3]

    Do not fear, for I am with you; I will bring your offspring from the east, and gather you from the west. I will say to the north, "Give them up!" And to the south, "Do not hold them back." Bring My sons from afar and My daughters from the ends of the earth (Isaiah 43:5-6).

    "Therefore behold, days are coming," declares the Lord, "when it will no longer be said, 'As the Lord lives, who brought up the sons of Israel out of the land of Egypt,' but, 'As the Lord lives, who brought up the sons of Israel from the land of the north and from all the countries where He had banished them.' For I will restore them to their own land which I gave to their fathers" (Jeremiah 16:14-15).

    "Behold, I am bringing them from the north country, and I will gather them from the remote parts of the earth, among them the blind and the lame, the woman

with child and she who is in labor with child, together; a great company, they will return here. "With weeping they will come, and by supplication I will lead them; I will make them walk by streams of waters, on a straight path in which they will not stumble; for I am a father to Israel, and Ephraim is My firstborn." Hear the word of the Lord, O nations, and declare in the coastlands afar off, and say, "He who scattered Israel will gather him and keep him as a shepherd keeps his flock" (Jeremiah 31:8-10).

"Therefore behold, the days are coming," declares the Lord, "when they will no longer say, 'As the Lord lives, who brought up the sons of Israel from the land of Egypt,' but, 'As the Lord lives, who brought up and led back the descendants of the household of Israel from the north land and from all the countries where I had driven them.' Then they will live on their own soil" (Jeremiah 23:7-8).

Then it will happen on that day that the Lord will again recover the second time with His hand the remnant of His people....And He will...assemble the banished ones of Israel, and will gather the dispersed of Judah from the four corners of the earth (Isaiah 11:11-12).

"For behold, days are coming," declares the Lord, "when I will restore the fortunes of My people Israel and Judah." The Lord says, "I will also bring them back to the land that I gave to their forefathers and they shall possess it" (Jeremiah 30:3).

For thus says the Lord, "Sing aloud with gladness for Jacob, and shout among the chief of the nations; proclaim, give praise and say, 'O Lord, save Your people, the remnant of Israel'" (Jeremiah 31:7).

C. Proclaim, praise, pray. These are our clear biblical mandates.

II. Understanding God's Plan for Israel

A. Romans 11:25-32:

For I do not want you, brethren, to be uninformed of this mystery—so that you will not be wise in your own estimation—that a partial hardening has happened to Israel until the fullness of the Gentiles has come in; and so all Israel will be saved; just as it is written, "The Deliverer will come from Zion, He will remove ungodliness from Jacob. This is my covenant with them, when I take away their sins." From the standpoint of the gospel they are enemies for your sake, but from the standpoint of God's choice they are beloved for the sake of the fathers; for the gifts and the calling of God are irrevocable. For just as you once were disobedient to God, but now have been shown mercy because of their disobedience, so these also now have been disobedient, that because of the mercy shown to you they also may now be shown mercy. For God has shut up all in disobedience so that He may show mercy to all.

B. Three key points:

1. All Israel, at some point, will be saved and brought to fullness.

And I will pour on the house of David and on the inhabitants of Jerusalem the Spirit of grace and supplication; then they will look on Me whom they pierced. Yes, they will mourn for Him as one mourns for his only son, and grieve for Him as one grieves for a firstborn. In that day there shall be a great mourning in Jerusalem, like the mourning at Hadad Rimmon in the plain of Megiddo (Zechariah 12:10-11 NKJV).

2. The Jewish people have a spirit of blindness as it relates to seeing their Messiah. For the past 2,000 years, the Gentiles have been able to take their blinders off, becoming believers in the Messiah and therefore God's "primary" instrument for the establishment of His Kingdom, working to bring the Gospel to all nations before the Second Coming of Christ. Gentile believers will rise up in prayer and supplication, and mighty waves of God's mercy will flow in the Land of Promise.

3. The blinders of the Jewish people will be removed when "the fullness of the Gentiles" is ushered in. The phrase *the fullness of the Gentiles* has several dimensions. First, it refers to the full number of Gentile converts written in the Lamb's Book of Life (see Rev. 7:9; 21:27). The term *fullness* also signifies the unprecedented release of the Holy Spirit's power at the end of the age, which will result in a harvest of souls unsurpassed in human history.

C. God's plan: God wants to use believers who carry a burden for the Jewish people to win to Jesus all the descendants of Abraham—Jews, Arabs, Chaldeans, and residents of the Middle East. "For the earth will be filled with the knowledge of the glory of the Lord, as the waters cover the sea" (Hab. 2:14).

III. The Church's Call to Stand With the Jewish People

A. Gentile believers must stand with the Jewish people. God's primary strategy to win the hearts of the Jewish people is through a compassionate and zealous Gentile Church. Paul defines this call as *"provoking them to jealousy"* (see Rom. 11:11 NKJV). This means that the reality of a Gentile Church, walking in authentic, compassionate, spiritual authority, will be extremely inviting and attractive to the Jewish people, which in turn will cause them to desire a deeper relationship with God by receiving their Messiah.

B. Paul warns the Church about the consequences of being spiritually ignorant about God's heart for the Jewish people.

But if some of the branches were broken off, and you, being a wild olive, were grafted in among them and became partaker with them of the rich root of the olive tree, do not be arrogant toward the branches; but if you are arrogant, remember that it is not you who supports the root, but the root supports you. You will say then, "Branches were broken off so that I might be grafted in." Quite right, they were broken off for their unbelief, but you stand by your faith. Do not be conceited, but fear; for if God did not spare the natural branches, He will not spare you, either. Behold then the kindness and severity of God; to those who fell, severity, but to you, God's kindness, if you continue in His kindness; otherwise you also will be cut off (Romans 11:17-22).

C. Jesus appealed to Gentile believers not to forsake His Jewish people during their time of great trouble. Those who choose to disregard the Lord's appeal and refuse to lend assistance to His people during her darkest hour will do so at their own spiritual peril. (See Matthew 25:31-42.)

IV. Praying for Jerusalem Is God's Desire for all Believers

A. Praying for the peace of Jerusalem is God's call for the entire Church.

I was glad when they said to me, "Let us go into the house of the Lord." Our feet have been standing within your gates, O Jerusalem! Jerusalem is built as a city that is compact together, where the tribes go up, the tribes of the Lord, to the Testimony of Israel, to give thanks to the name of the Lord. For thrones are set there for judgment, the thrones of the house of David. Pray for the peace of Jerusalem: "May they prosper who love you. Peace be within your walls, prosperity within your palaces." For the sake of my brethren and companions, I will now say, "Peace be within you." Because of the house of the Lord our God I will seek your good (Psalm 122 NKJV).

1. God commands His people to "give Him no rest" until Jerusalem enters into the fullness of her inheritance. The peace of Jerusalem refers to Israel entering into the fullness of her destiny as spoken by the Old Testament prophets. "I have set watchmen on your walls, O

Jerusalem; they shall never hold their peace day or night. You who make mention of the Lord, do not keep silent, and give Him no rest till He establishes and till He makes Jerusalem a praise in the earth" (Isa. 62:6-7 NKJV).

2. God is calling the Church to give herself in fervent intercession for the salvation of Israel and for the transformation of a dusty, Middle Eastern town into a city that will show forth the very glory of God.

B. Praying for Jerusalem means partnership with God.

1. When we pray for Jerusalem, we link ourselves with God, who is consumed with zeal for this city. We stand with Israel in the place of prayer because we love Jesus, and we want to share His heart.

2. The prophet Zechariah saw a vision that depicted the oppressed state of Israel. In response, the Angel of the Lord (the pre-incarnate Christ) lifted His voice to declare, "How long will you not have mercy on Jerusalem?" An answer comes from the throne, and it describes the heart and affections of God for this nation that has recently returned from captivity:

Thus says the Lord of hosts, "I am exceedingly jealous for Jerusalem and Zion. But I am very angry with the nations who are at ease; for while I was only a little angry, they furthered the disaster." Therefore thus says the Lord, "I will return to Jerusalem with compassion; My house will be built in it," declares the Lord of hosts, "and a measuring line will be stretched over Jerusalem" (Zechariah 1:14-16).

3. Everything that God says and does is for the sake of fulfilling His promises toward Jerusalem. "For Zion's sake I will not keep silent, and for Jerusalem's sake I will not keep quiet, until her righteousness goes forth like brightness, and her salvation like a torch that is burning" (Isa. 62:1).

4. God is declaring that this little piece of real estate is not insignificant; rather, it is the object of His fiery affection. He is zealous for this contested city in the Middle East.

C. Praying for Jerusalem means contending for Israel's salvation.

1. The return of Jesus to Jerusalem is contingent upon Israel's acceptance of their Messiah, Jesus.

*"O Jerusalem, Jerusalem, you who kill the prophets and stone those sent to you, how often I have longed to gather your children together, as a hen gathers her chicks under her wings, but you were not willing. Look, your house is left to you desolate. For I tell you, **you will not see Me again until you say, 'Blessed is He who comes in the name of the Lord'"** (Matthew 23:37-39 NIV).*

2. In the days following Pentecost, Peter's sermons (see Acts 2:36; 3:12,19) called the nation of Israel and the leaders of Jerusalem to repentance and faith in Jesus so that "your sins may be blotted out...that He may send Jesus Christ who was preached to you before" (Acts 3:19-20 NKJV).

3. Israel's acceptance of Jesus as her Messiah depends on her being provoked to jealousy by a predominantly Gentile Church (see Rom. 11:11,30-32). The Church's role as a prophetic witness is directly related to her stand for Jerusalem in the place of prayer.

D. Praying for Jerusalem is God's strategy to release fullness to the Gentiles and mercy to the Jewish people.

   1. Right away also, satan launched an all-out assault on the nation of Israel and the city of Jerusalem. He knows that Jesus committed Himself to returning as King of the Jews, to rule the earth from Jerusalem (see Matt. 23:39).

   2. If satan can annihilate the Jewish people, he can prove God to be a liar and ensure his own survival. So he attempts to rally the nations of the earth to his cause. Global anti-Semitism is the result. In our own lifetimes, we may see the time when every nation of the earth actively seeks the destruction of Jerusalem under the leadership of a world leader commonly known as the antichrist. (See First John 4:3; Zechariah 12:2; 14:2, Zephaniah 3:7-8.)

   3. As the saints of God partner with Him in prayer and in solidarity with Israel, He promises to do two things in response.

      a. He will release His voice in the earth (the "spirit of prophecy"). The spirit of prophecy is the testimony of Jesus (see Rev. 19:10). The testimony of Jesus results in revival among the Gentiles, which will provoke Israel to jealousy.

b. He will release supernatural activity in the earth (judgments against His enemies). He wants righteousness to prevail (see Isa. 62:1-2), and He will raise up messengers who will proclaim with boldness, authority, and clarity the "Gospel of the Kingdom" (see Matt. 24:14), especially to the Jewish people in the midst of tribulation. He will release signs and wonders as evidence of His coming again (see Joel 2:30-31).

E. Salvation and deliverance in Jerusalem: "And it shall come to pass that whoever calls on the name of the Lord shall be saved. For in Mount Zion and in Jerusalem there shall be deliverance, as the Lord has said, among the remnant whom the Lord calls" (Joel 2:32 NKJV).

1. The end result of God's activity is the deliverance of Jerusalem from her enemies, the salvation of "all Israel," and the establishing of God's Kingdom on the earth in fullness. "And so all Israel will be saved, as it is written: 'The Deliverer will come out of Zion, and He will turn away ungodliness from Jacob; for this is My covenant with them, when I take away their sins'" (Rom. 11:26-27 NKJV).

2. God's end-time activity is released out of His zeal for Jerusalem and because of God's people lining up with His heart and praying for the salvation of Israel with fasting and solemn assemblies across the earth.

Blow a trumpet in Zion, consecrate a fast, proclaim a solemn assembly, gather the people, sanctify the congregation, assemble the elders, gather the children and the nursing infants. Let the bridegroom come out of his room and the bride out of her bridal chamber. Let the priests, the Lord's ministers, weep between the porch and the altar, and let them say, "Spare Your people, O Lord, and do not make Your inheritance a reproach, a byword among the nations" (Joel 2:15-17).

3. The ultimate task of the Gentile Church is to pray for the salvation of Israel and to provoke the Jews to jealousy (by becoming a powerful prophetic witness) so that they will receive the mercy of God.

Summary

Ever since 1967, when war in the Middle East brought Jerusalem under the control of the Jewish people as the state of Israel, the dispensation of the Gentiles began to shift in a significant way. Jerusalem is becoming the last-days epicenter for God's activity in the earth. When you can grasp this with your eyes and heart, and when you join your voice and your efforts with others, you become an end-time harvester.

Reflection Questions

Lesson 12: Praying Effectively for Israel

(Answers to these questions can be found in the back of the study guide.)

1. "The _____ fervent prayer of a righteous man availeth much" (James 5:16 KJV).

2. What does *aliyah* mean? What is its significance to the salvation of the Jewish people?

3. What are the three key points to remember about understanding God's plan for Israel? (See II.B.1–3.)

   a. _____

   b _____

   c _____

4. Cite two or three Scripture passages that indicate the role of the Gentile Church in God's plan for the Jewish people.

   _____

   _____

   _____

5. Now state in your own words the role of the Gentile Church in God's plan for the Jewish people.

   _____

   _____

PERSONAL APPLICATION QUESTION

6. Do you "pray for the peace of Jerusalem"? If so, how can you pray more effectively? If not, how can you make a start?

_____

_____

_____

_____

_____

_____

_____

_____

ANSWERS TO REFLECTION QUESTIONS

LESSON 1: "PRAYER STORM"—WHAT IS IT?

1. cry

2. fire, altar

3. *inter, cedere*, stand

4. harp, bowls

5. distances, balanced, fresh, fire

LESSON 2: WALKING IN THE FOOTSTEPS OF JESUS

1. (a) His earthly prayer life, (b) His position at the right hand of God the Father, (c) His ongoing activity in Heaven.

3. Yes. (We see his emotion portrayed in the Bible, e.g. John 11:33-38, the raising of Lazarus.)

4. burden

LESSON 3: SPIRIT-EMPOWERED PRAYER STORM

1. (a) prophetic intercession, (b) revelatory prayer

2. prophet, priest

4. tongues

5. travail

LESSON 4: INTERCESSORY PRAYER STORM IN TIMES OF CRISIS

2. (a) cry for mercy, (b) authoritative intercession, (c) repentance.

3. blessing

5. crisis

LESSON 5: PRAYER WITH FASTING—GOD'S WAY

1. food

2. aligns (or unites)

4. prayer

LESSON 6: SOAKING IN HIS PRESENCE

1. relationship

4. presence

LESSON 7: TAPPING THE POWER OF HIGH PRAISE

1. God's, God's

2. (a) as a means of deliverance, (b) as a means to silence the devil, (c) as the way into Christ's victory.

4. thanksgiving

5. the dead

LESSON 8: PRAYER FOR REVIVAL IN THE CHURCH

2. (a) prayer, (b) networking (unity with others).

3. (a) an experiential conviction of sin, (b) a passionate denunciation of sin, (c) a revelation of God's holiness, (d) a deep awareness of God's love and mercy, (e) a sometimes painfully heightened consciousness of eternity.

4. prayer

5. persecution

LESSON 9: PRAYER FOR ANOTHER GREAT AWAKENING—YOUTH

3. Prophetic

4. (three of the following reasons): 24/7 worship and prayer…

    a. …is done in Heaven and therefore should be done on earth

    b. …releases God's justice on the earth

    c. …fuels the Great Commission

    d. …hinders the plans of the devil

    e. …releases revival breakthrough

    f. …prepares the way for Christ's second coming

LESSON 10: PRAYING YOUR FAMILY INTO THE KINGDOM

1. family (kindred, clan)

2. (see Lesson Ten, II.)

3. families

4. household

5. (see Lesson Ten, IV. A–J)

LESSON 11: PRAYING FOR PEOPLE IN AUTHORITY

1. authority, saved

2. (a) "So that we may lead a tranquil and quiet life in all godliness and dignity"; (b) So that God can save all men and bring them to a knowledge of the truth.

3. righteousness

4. See I.E.3.a–j. for all ten ways to pray for people in authority.

LESSON 12: PRAYING EFFECTIVELY FOR ISRAEL

1. effectual (effective)

2. *Aliyah* means the "ascent" or the "return to the land."

3. (a) All Israel at some point will be saved and brought to fullness; (b) The Jewish people have a spirit of blindness as it relates to seeing their Messiah; (c) The blinders of the Jewish people will be removed when "the fullness of the Gentiles" is ushered in.

Appendixes

Appendix A

PRAYER STORM

ONE-HOUR PRAYER GUIDE

This guide is intended to be only an outline, surrendered to the leading of the Holy Spirit as a flexible tool to help you in your hour of worship and intercession as part of Prayer Storm. It is not a formula, and you do not have to follow it to the letter. Your times of prayer may vary greatly from one week to the next, as the Spirit leads you. Below, you will find a brief outline, followed by further explanation.

60-MINUTE OUTLINE FOR PRAYER STORM PRAYER

- Read the current Prayer Storm Prayer Alert—2 minutes

- Offer thanksgiving and praise—3 minutes

- Sing and pray in the Spirit—5 minutes

- Read Scripture—5 minutes

- Pray for revival in the Church—10 minutes

- Sing and pray in the Spirit—5 minutes

- Pray for Israel—10 minutes

- Sing and pray in the Spirit—5 minutes

- Pray for a youth awakening—10 minutes

- Offer thanksgiving and praise—5 minutes

A Few Instructions

Based on this outline, here are a few simple instructions to help you make your time effective.

Weekly Prayer Alerts will be sent out to each Prayer Storm participant. They will be posted also on the Prayer Storm Website (www.prayerstorm.com). Please begin by reading the current Prayer Alert. Then proceed to offer thanksgiving and praise to the Lord. Remember, Psalm 100 instructs us to enter into His gates with thanksgiving and into His courts with praise. You can enter God's throne room with thanksgiving and praise! If you find music helpful, play an instrument or use an instrumental worship CD in the background. Do whatever will make your time the most effective.

One of the emphases of Prayer Storm is upon Spirit-led and Spirit-empowered worship and prayer. Therefore, consider singing and praying in the Holy Spirit or praying by using the gift of tongues (see 1 Cor. 14) as a part of your time. If you have not yet been released into this dimension of prayer, do not worry. You can participate by simply worshiping the Lord periodically throughout your hour. Remember, the Lord inhabits the praises of His people. You are one of His people, and He will inhabit your praises.

It is vital to be Spirit-led and Word-grounded in your times of intercession. Every so often, the Prayer Alert will direct you to read a Scripture passage that will fuel your faith. At other times, it will be left up to you to select a short portion of the Bible to read.

As you proceed into the current "burdens or themes" in prayer, make it practical. Call out to the Lord for revival in the Church. Pray for your region and nation and the church in your city to come alive in Jesus' name! As you proceed through the theme(s) for that week, remember that the Website incorporates Scripture-based teaching outlines for every area or emphasis: revival in the Church, prayer for Israel, youth awakening, and crisis intercession. Avail yourself of these tools, as they will help you hit the mark in your prayers.

While the outline lists the different prayer themes in a certain order, giving each subject a few minutes, you should be aware that the Holy Spirit might "land on" one of them, such as revival in the Church, and you will not be able to get away from it. That is great! Follow His lead; that is the goal. Other times, you will not be aware of a particular leading of the Spirit, so you will simply pray through this outline or one that you have devised. Either way is good. Just be faithful in your hourly watch.

Also note that crisis intercession does not appear as a special section in this prayer outline. That is because special notices for crisis intercession will be e-mailed out whenever necessary. Again, there might be times when your entire hour or another day or hour will be spent entirely on crisis intercession. That is wonderful. Intercessors are to be flexible instruments in the Lord's hand.

You will notice that the outline keeps coming back to singing and praying in the Spirit. This is important! Your faith will be charged, and your prayers will then be supernaturally guided if you worship the Lord and pray in the Spirit frequently.

You will also notice that the hour not only begins with thanksgiving and praise, it also ends with it. Thank Him and praise Him for His answers to your prayers. Thank Him and praise Him that He is raising up intercessors all over the globe. Rejoice that the fire of the Moravian lampstand is not going out and that the continuous chorus of prayer is swelling even as you speak. Offer up a shout if you want. Thank the Lord that He has heard you and many other intercessors around the globe who are taking their place as watchmen on the walls for such a time as this.

May these simple guidelines help you to have an effective time in your Prayer Storm assignment!

Prayer Storm—Restoring and Releasing the Global Moravian Lampstand

The fire shall ever be burning upon the altar; it shall never go out (Leviticus 6:13 KJV).

(For an online version of this prayer guide, go to the Prayer Storm Website: http://www.prayerstorm.com/1hour_outline.html)

Appendix B

Resources for Intercessors

This is not an exhaustive list. On many of the recommended Websites, you will find links to other helpful organizations, as well as extensive lists of books about intercessory prayer and the Prayer Storm themes of prayer emphasis, revival, youth awakening, Israel, and crisis intercession.

24-7 Prayer (www.24-7prayer.com/cm/resources/288)

Pete Greig, who formerly worked with Jackie Pullinger in Hong Kong, is now an author, a church-planter, and the international director of 24-7 Prayer, which has grown in eight years from a single 24-7 prayer room based on the Moravian model into an "international, interdenominational youth movement committed to prayer, mission and justice."

Aglow International (www.aglow.org)

Since Aglow was formed in 1967, it has been known as a network of caring, praying women. Now 172 nations strong, Aglow can rapidly mobilize via e-mail more than one million intercessors worldwide who understand the power of strategic prayer.

Bound4Life (http://bound4life.com)

Along with others, pray a short prayer, frequently and effectively: "Jesus, I plead your blood over my sins and the sins of my nation; God, end abortion, and send revival to America." Participate in silent prayer "seiges." See Website for more information and for resources such as a prayer-reminder wristband.

TheCall (www.thecall.com)

Spearheaded by Lou Engle, these are stadium events that are *not* merely concerts but are rather, in their words—"A fast, not a festival" and "a massive gathering of young and old who are desperate for a revival in our nation." On the Website, you will find a news feed, information about upcoming gatherings, resources, and more.

Campus Church Networks (http://campuschurch.net)

Campus Transformation Network (http://campustransformation.com)

Jaeson Ma (www.jaesonma.com) is a 20-something Chinese American with a passion for Jesus. He leads a growing campus ministry, and he is the author of *The Blueprint: A Revolutionary Plan to Plant Missional Communities on Campus.*

The Daily Brief (http://chpponline.blogspot.com/)

"The Daily Brief" is a daily news alert sent free by e-mail to subscribers. It is published by Capitol Hill Prayer Partners (CHPP), which is a ministry dedicated to praying for U.S. leaders and for issues involving national security. Their Website includes many links to other organizations and ministries.

Daily Text (Bible verses and prayers for each day of the year)

Bible texts are selected annually by the Moravian Church and shared world wide—since 1731! This rich source of personal renewal is produced fresh each year by praying and believing Moravian Christians. Order it in a book form or get it free via email.

> Mount Carmel Ministries
> 800 Mount Carmel Drive NE
> PO Box 579
> Alexandria, MN 56308
> Phone: 320-846-2744 or 1-800-793-4311
> Fax: 320-846-0067
> Website: www.dailytext.com

For an e-mail devotional version of Daily Text sent directly to you each day contact: ministries@dailytext.com.

DAY TO PRAY FOR THE PEACE OF JERUSALEM (HTTP://WWW.JERUSALEMPRAYERBANQUET.COM/)

The International Day of Prayer for the Peace of Jerusalem is held annually on the first Sunday of October, coinciding with the season of Yom Kippur. It is one of the initiatives of Robert Stearns, Eagles' Wings executive director.

EVERY HOME FOR CHRIST (WWW.EHC.ORG)

Find books and other resources, such as a World Prayer Map, on their Website. Every Home for Christ and its Jericho Center of Prayer are chaired by national prayer leader Dick Eastman.

GLOBAL DAY OF PRAYER (WWW.GLOBALDAYOFPRAYER.COM/)

From South Africa, Graham Powells coordinates a multi-nation day of prayer. The Website, which includes links to the GDoP sites of dozens of countries, gives details of past events and the current year's events. The key Scripture for the GDoP is Second Chronicles 7:14: "If my people, who are called by My name, will humble themselves and pray...."

HARVEST PRAYER MINISTRIES (WWW.HARVESTPRAYER.COM)

Harvest Prayer Ministries was formed "to equip the local church to become a House of Prayer for all nations, releasing God's power for revival and finishing the task of world evangelization." Follow a link to an extensive online prayer-themed bookshop called PrayerShop.

INCREASE INTERNATIONAL (WWW.INTERCESSORSINTERNATIONAL.ORG/)

Elizabeth (Beth) Alves assembles intercessors for teaching and united prayer. Her books include *Intercessors: Discovering Your Prayer Power* and *Becoming a Prayer Warrior.*

INTERCESSORS FOR AMERICA (WWW.IFAPRAY.ORG)

This site and free subscription-only e-mails contain a wealth of up-to-date information about national and international prayer needs, including those of Israel.

IFA partners with many other organizations, and you can find links to their Web-sites on the IFA site, including the following sites which may be of particular interest to Prayer Storm intercessors: America's National Prayer Committee, The U.S. Prayer Center, Mission America, Campus Renewal Ministries, See You at the Pole (youth), and more. Over 300 books about prayer and prayer-related issues are available through IFA.

INTERNATIONAL HOUSE OF PRAYER (IHOP) (WWW.IHOP.ORG/GROUP/GROUP.ASPX?ID=14025)

From Kansas City, Missouri, Mike Bickle and his team coordinate 24/7 worship and intercession. The Website is a rich source of prayer resources, including information about conferences, Webcasts and podcasts, Nightwatch, the Israel Mandate, and the Global Bridegroom Fast.

ISRAEL PRAYER COALITION (WWW.ENCOUNTERSNETWORK.COM/ISRAEL_PRAYER_COALITION)

James W. Goll networks with ministries of intercession, compassion, and humanitarian aid to Israel, coordinating and releasing strategic calls to prayer, including the The Cry (prayer and fasting during Purim each year). The Coalition also hosts prayer-focused tours to Israel.

JERUSALEM HOUSE OF PRAYER FOR ALL NATIONS (WWW.JHOPFAN.ORG)

Tom Hess is the president of this organization, the motto of which is "Proclaim…Pray…Praise." He leads prayer tours of Israel, prayer convocations, the Watchman's School of Ministry, and the All Nations World Wide Watch Jerusalem, which proclaim, praise, and pray for the peace of Jerusalem through the twelve gates of the city.

LUKE 18 PROJECT (WWW.LUKE18PROJECT.COM)

Directed by Brian Kim and closely affiliated with TheCall (Lou Engle), the Luke 18 Project has a goal of planting 24/7 prayer rooms on every college campus—as many as 10,000 of them. It is based on Luke 18:6-7: "And the Lord said, …'Will not God bring about justice for his chosen ones, who cry out to him day and night?'"

MOMS IN TOUCH (WWW.MOMSINTOUCH.ORG)

Founded and directed by Fern Nichols in 1984 and growing quickly because of exposure on Focus on the Family, today Moms In Touch has groups in all 50 states as well as representatives in over 120 foreign countries. They pray weekly for their children and their schools.

MORAVIAN HYMNS

Historic Moravian hymns have been translated into English. *The Moravian Book of Worship* is available from the Moravian Church (which celebrated its 550-year anniversary in 2007) at www.moravian.org/publications/catalog. *The Companion to the Moravian Book of Worship* is available from the Moravian Music Foundation at www.moravianmusic.org/books.html.

NATIONAL DAY OF PRAYER (WWW.NDPTF.ORG)

This national day of prayer for America's leaders and families exists because of a presidential decree, and it operates under the authority of the President of the United States. The National Day of Prayer itself is held annually on the first Thursday of May, and a year-round task force mobilizes participation and maintains communication.

NATIONAL GOVERNMENTAL PRAYER ALLIANCE (WWW.NATIONALGPA.ORG)

Established by Dutch Sheets, the NGPA networks with other Christian organizations and serves as a "clearinghouse for information on the activities of our three branches of government at the national and state levels, enabling the Body of Christ to pray more effectively and to act responsibly and proactively to see governmental change." They also teach about effective intercession, making "every attempt to be prophetic and proactive as opposed to responsive and defensive" in their prayer activities.

PRAYER CENTRAL (WWW.PRAYERCENTRAL.NET)

This is a Web-based source of inspiration and information about prayer for national and international concerns, Israel, and much more.

PRAYER MOUNTAIN (WWW.FGTV.ORG/N_ENGLISH/PRAYER/P_INDEX.ASP)

The Osanri Choi Ja-Shil Memorial Fasting Prayer Mountain, Osanri, Kyonggi Province, Korea was founded by David Yonggi Cho's Yoidi Full Gospel Church of Seoul, South Korea. The Prayer Mountain can accomodate up to 10,000 people at one time for private and corporate prayer. (See also www.davidcho.com/NewEng/PrayerMountain.asp.)

PRAYER STORM (WWW.PRAYERSTORM.COM)

Keep up with the latest postings from James W. Goll and the Prayer Storm team. Sign up for your hour of prayer. (After only the first two months, 1,400 intercessors from 40 nations have signed up, taking one hour of prayer per week. The goal is one million intercessors praying around the clock, around the world for specific crises, revival in the Church, a youth awakening, and Israel!)

REFORMATION PRAYER NETWORK (WWW.GENERALS.ORG)

Founded by Mike and Cindy Jacobs of Generals International (formerly Generals of Intercession), the Reformation Prayer Network pulls together the apostolic, prophetic, and intercessory movements to more effectively bring the transformational power of the Kingdom of God to earth today.

SUCCAT HALLEL (WWW.JERUSALEMPRAISE.COM)

Succat Hallel means "Tabernacle of Praise" in Hebrew, and since 1999, Rick and Patti Ridings have hosted 24/7 prayer and praise in the city of Jerusalem. The primary facility of Succat Hallel overlooks Mount Zion and the Old City of Jerusalem.

WATCH OF THE LORD (WWW.MAHESHCHAVDA.COM/WOTL.ASP)

This is a global prayer movement begun by Mahesh and Bonnie Chavda in 1995. Up to a thousand believers ("watchmen") gather at the Watch headquarters in Charlotte, North Carolina, every Friday night to spend the entire night in worship and prayer. Other locations host similar gatherings. Individuals can participate in the Watch of the Lord via webcast.

ENDNOTES

LESSON 1

1. *Merriam-Webster's Collegiate Dictionary*, 11th ed., s.v. "Prayer"; see also *Shorter Oxford English Dictionary, Sixth Edition*.

2. *Merriam Webster's Collegiate Dictionary*, 11th ed., s.v. "Storm"; see also *Shorter Oxford English Dictionary, Sixth Edition*.

3. *Merriam-Webster's Collegiate Dictionary*, 11th ed., "Intercede."

4. *Merriam-Webster's Collegiate Dictionary*, 11th ed., s.v.v. "Intercession," "Intercede"; see also *Shorter Oxford English Dictionary, Sixth Edition*.

5. "Entugchano"; see http://www.studylight.org/lex/grk/view.cgi?number=1793; this resource uses *Thayer's and Smith's Bible Dictionary* and the *Theological Dictionary of the New Testament*.

6. "Paga"; see http://www.studylight.org/lex/heb/view.cgi?number=06293; this resource uses the *Brown-Driver-Briggs-Gesenius Lexicon* and the *Theological Word Book of the Old Testament*.

7. Facts for this section have been gleaned from "Zinzendorf: the Count Without Borders," the official site of the Zinzendorf documentary series from the Comenius Foundation, at http://www.zinzendorf.com/countz.htm; and from Leslie K. Tarr, "The Prayer Meeting that Lasted 100 Years," *Christian History*, no. 1 (1997): http://www.ctlibrary.com/3263.

LESSON 2

1. *Strong's Exhaustive Concordance of the Bible*, "embrimaomai," 1690.

2. Charles Haddon Spurgeon, *Twelve Sermons on Prayer* (London: Marshall, Morgan, & Scott, n.d.), 39.

3. "Nasa"; see http://www.studylight.org/lex/heb/view.cgi?number=05375.

4. *Strong's Exhaustive Concordance of the Bible,* "bastazo," 941.

5. "Anechomai"; see http://www.studylight.org/lex/grk/view.cgi?number=430.

6. Wesley Duewel, *Mighty Prevailing Prayer* (Grand Rapids, MI: Zondervan, 1990), 40-41.

LESSON 3

1. *Merriam-Webster's Collegiate Dictionary,* 11th ed., s.v. "Conspire"; from Latin "conspirare." "Breathed" or "Naphach"; http://www.studylight.org/lex/heb/view.cgi?number=05301.

2. "Genos"; see http://www.studylight.org/lex/grk/view.cgi?number=1085.

3. "Groanings"; http://www.studylight.org/lex/grk/view.cgi?number=4726.

4. *Merriam-Webster's Collegiate Dictionary,* 11th ed., s.v. "Fervent."

LESSON 5

1. "Tsum"; see http://www.studylight.org/lex/heb/view.cgi?number=06684.

2. Epiphanius of Salamis, quoted in John Wesley, "Causes of the Inefficacy of Christianity," sermon 116, Dublin, July 2, 1789.

3. Elmer L. Towns, *Fasting for Spiritual Breakthrough: A Guide to Nine Biblical Fasts* (Ventura, CA: Regal, 1996), 22ff.

4. Arthur Wallis, *God's Chosen Fast* (Fort Washington, PA: Christian Literature Crusade, 1968), 25-26.

5. See Lou Engle, *Fast Forward* (Washington, DC: cu@dc, 1999).

LESSON 8

1. Colin Dye, teaching notes, quoted in James W. Goll, *Revival Breakthrough Study Guide* (Franklin, TN: Encounters Network, 2000), 43. Colin Dye is a scholar and statesman as well as the pastor of Kensington Temple in London, England, one of the largest churches in Europe.

2. The story of the Hebrides Revival has been published in many places. You can read a transcript of an account delivered by Duncan Campbell in 1968 on the

Website of Shilohouse Ministries at http://www.shilohouse.org/Hebrides_Revival.htm.

3. J. Edwin Orr, "The Role of Prayer in Spiritual Awakening," http://www.jedwinorr.com/prayer_revival.htm.

4. Charles Finney, for this description of revival, see "What a Revival of Religion Is," http://www.gospeltruth.net/1868Lect_on_Rev_of_Rel/68revlec01.htm.

5. From commentary on Isaiah 62:6-9; Matthew Henry, *Commentary on the Whole Bible, Vol. IV (Isaiah to Malachi)*, 2nd ed, (Peabody, MA: Hendrickson Publishers, 1991).

6. Leonard Ravenhill, *Why Revival Tarries* (Bloomington, MN: Bethany House, 1979), 138.

7. E. M. Bounds, *The Necessity of Prayer* (Grand Rapids, MI: Baker, 1979), 63.

LESSON 9

1. Jaeson Ma, *The Blueprint* (Ventura, CA: Regal, 2007), 35-36.

2. Ibid.

3. Stephen Ross, "Charles Thomas (C.T.) Studd," *Worldwide Missions: Mission Biographies*, http://www.wholesomewords.org/missions/biostudd.html (accessed 21 April 2008).

4. "Campus Ministry Cambridge Style," *Christian History & Biography*, no 88 (2005), 13. For more on this subject, consult these books: *Revival Fire*, by Wesley Duewel, *The Classics on Revival*, by Robert Backhouse, Campus Aflame, by J. Edwin Orr, and *Revival: Its Principles and Personalities*, by Winkie Pratney.

5. Steve Shadrach, "5 Students Who Changed the World," *Boundless Webzine*, (2003), http://www.boundless.org/2002_2003/regulars/list_guy/a0000739.html (accessed 21 April 2008).

6. Paul Van Der Werf, "Haystack Reloaded: Could a Haystack Change the World Again?" *Student Volunteer Movement 2*, http://www.svm2.citymaker.com/haystackreloaded.html (accessed 21 April 2008).

7. Ma, 107-110.

8. J. Edwin Orr, "Prayer and Revival," www.jedewinorr.com/prayer_revival.htm (accessed May 2007), quoted in Ma, *The Blueprint*.

LESSON 11

1. Andrew Murray, *Helps to Intercession* (Fort Washington, PA: Christian Literature Crusade, 2007), Day 17.

2. Jack W. Hayford, *Prayer Is Invading the Impossible* (New York: Ballantine Books, 1983), 57.

3. In ancient Middle Eastern cities, a city would have more than one gate, and they were connected by broad walls (which you could compare to the "walls of salvation). At least three offices would be represented or contained at the gateways of a city: commercial, judicial, and prophetic. Actual real estate transactions were handled at the gateway; deeds were transferred, signatures were collected. Court cases and judicial hearings were held right in the gate, and decisions would be announced right there. In addition, prophetic words, the Word of the Lord, would be delivered to the priests in the gate (see Prov. 1:21; Jer. 17:19-20; 26:10,13). So there at the gate, a person would find commerce moving, the justice system operating, and spiritual dynamics taking place.

4. Bruce P. Stark, "Thomas Hooker," *Connecticut's Heritage Gateway*, www.ctheritage.org, quoted in Derek Prince, *Shaping History Through Prayer and Fasting* (New Kensington, PA: Whitaker House, 2002).

5. Thomas Hooker, quoted in Alden T. Vaughan, The Puritan Tradition in America, 1620–1730 (Lebanon, NH: University Press of New England, 1997), 84.

6. Daniel Webster, quoted in Prince, *Shaping History Through Prayer and Fasting*.

7. Charles Stanley, see http://www.eagleforum.org/court_watch/reports/2001/6-27-01/pray-for-govt-officials.shtml.

LESSON 12

1. "Energeo"; http://www.studylight.org/lex/grk/view.cgi?number=1754.

2. Aliyah"; http://www.studylight.org/lex/heb/view.cgi?number=05944.

3. Joel Brinkley, "Ethiopian Jews and Israelis Exult as Airlift Is Completed," *The New York Times*, May 26, 1991, http://query.nytimes.com/gst/fullpage.html?res=9D0CE2DD1E3CF935A15756C0A967958260&sec=&spon=&pagewanted=all (accessed 22 March 2008).

ABOUT THE AUTHOR

James (Jim) W. Goll is the cofounder of Encounters Network (formerly Ministry to the Nations) with his wife, Michal Ann. James also acts as the director of Prayer Storm, an internet-based virtual house of prayer. They are members of the Harvest International Ministries Apostolic Team and contributing writers for *Kairos* magazine and other periodicals. James and Michal Ann have four wonderful children and live in the beautiful, rolling hills of Franklin, Tennessee.

James has produced several study guides on subjects such as Equipping in the Prophetic, Blueprints for Prayer, and Empowered for Ministry, which are all available through the Encounters Resource Center.

Other books by James and Michal Ann Goll include:

A Call to Courage
Angelic Encounters
Call to the Secret Place
Compassion
The Beginner's Guide to Hearing God
The Coming Israel Awakening
The Coming Prophetic Revolution
The Prophetic Intercessor
Praying for Israel's Destiny

For more information, contact:

Encounters Network
P.O. Box 1653
Franklin, TN 37057
Office Phone: 615-599-5552
Office Fax: 615-599-5554
For orders call: 1-877-200-1604

For more information or to sign up for monthly e-mail communiqués, please visit www.encountersnetwork.com or send an e-mail to: info@encountersnetwork.com.

For more information on Prayer Storm, visit www.prayerstorm.com. You may sign up for an hour of prayer or view the weekly Webcast by visiting this Website.

Additional copies of this book and other book titles from DESTINY IMAGE are available at your local bookstore.

Call toll-free: 1-800-722-6774.

Send a request for a catalog to:

Destiny Image® Publishers, Inc.
P.O. Box 310
Shippensburg, PA 17257-0310

"Speaking to the Purposes of God for This Generation and for the Generations to Come."

**For a complete list of our titles,
visit us at www.destinyimage.com.**